Making Parenting Simple

A Parenting Guide Handbook

Mark Kovach

Copyright © 2019 Mark Kovach

No part of this book may be reproduced, stored in a retrieval system or transmitted by any mean without the permission of the author.

ISBN: 978-0-692-18063-1

ACKNOWLEDGEMENT AND DEDICATION

I would like to acknowledge and dedicate this book to my son and daughter, the two most wonderful children that any parent could have ever asked for. Both of my kids are grown now, but nevertheless, they have been great to have and raise as I watched them grow up to become very productive members of society. Not only did I learn a lot from them in the different developing stages of their lives, but I can only hope and pray that they learned a lot from me and from my incredibly patient and loving second wife who was there throughout their developing and growing up process. However, the one thing that took me awhile to learn (in years) was how much patience is required to raise children, but it turned out to be the simplest and easiest job that I have ever enjoyed doing. Both of my children were pretty much trained before birth, so I had very little to do in order to correct any problems that developed between the kids, but we will get to that in the very first chapter. Nevertheless, having two well-behaved kids made my life a lot nicer and much more enjoyable to have the kids around and not have to worry about them getting loud, out-of-hand, and causing or getting into trouble. After reading this book I hope people will learn how easy and simple it really is to raise well-rounded and balanced children in today's crazy world that we all try to get along, survive, and live in. Furthermore, I went out of my way to inform my children that my new wife would be my children's best friend. Also, she was not to be referred to as step mother or mother as they already had a mother and I also emphasized this to my new wife and she agreed. Because of this notification to my wife and children we have never encountered any problems in our family as long as we have been together even to this day concerning our relationships.

Contents

Acknowledgment And Dedication		iii
Introduction	Making Parenting Simple	vi
Chapter 1	Congratulations You're Gonna Have A Baby Or Babies	1
Chapter 2	The Positive Child	7
Chapter 3	The Endless Parent World Of Saying No	12
Chapter 4	The Positive Parents VS. The Negative Parents	18
Chapter 5	Correcting Children's Behavior Or Disciplining Children's Behavior	25
Part 2	What To Do When Things Really Go Wrong	31
Chapter 6	Children's Safety Training A Priority	40
Part 2	Training Observance And Password	42
Part 3	Reinforcing Awareness	45
Chapter 7	The Family Betrayal By Close Trusted Family Members And Friends	49
Chapter 8	Inappropriate Sexual Behavior	56
Part 2	Understanding With Correction And Explanation	59
Part 3	Break Time A Little About My Wife	61
Part 2	Continued	63
Chapter 9	Kids Are A Mirrored Reflection Of Their Parents	66
Part 2	The Destructive World Of Cell Phones	68
Part 3	Learning To Become Responsible	71
Chapter 10	Learning And Understanding Responsibility	75
Part 2	Raising Children To Be Efficient And Competent	84
Chapter 11	Welcome To The Wonderful World Of Lying	87
Chapter 12	How To Handle The Problem Child	91
Part 2	Sibling Rivalry	94

Part 3	Other Factors That Can Cause Problem Children	97
Chapter 13	A Parent's Worst Nightmare	103
Chapter 14	The Nightmare Gets Worse	111
Part 2	The Nightmare Continues	116
Chapter 15	More To Come	122
Chapter 16	Are Parents Just Bad Or Stupid	128
Part 2	Do Parents Raise Bullies	131
Chapter 17	What Kind Of Parents Will You Become	136
Chapter 18	The Bottom Line	141
Chapter 19	The Realities Of Being A Parent	146

INTRODUCTION

Making Parenting Simple

This book has been written for parents, but especially, expecting parents as well as new parents along with established parents who are interested in learning a simple way in which to train and raise their child or children in the very early stages of their developing lives from a fetus, to babies, to toddlers, and throughout their growing years. All of these events that are discussed in this book are true and factual and have been tried and tested and incorporated by the author that not only makes parenting simple, but also to aid parents by showing them how they can protect and guide their child or children from childhood to adulthood with different and effective parenting techniques. Notwithstanding, unlike the author who had to overcome the violence, cruelty, brutality, and viciousness he suffered because of the ways that his parents raised him and his brothers, he nevertheless managed to become a well-rounded business person despite all of the setbacks that he had to endure while growing up in his early childhood and teenage years.

Although the author was never taught any social skills by his parents and nor did he develop any meaningful social skills, it resulted in him becoming a solitary person and avoiding any desire to wanting to establish any sort of relationships outside of his immediate family. However, the author was determined to demonstrate to parents that there is a better way to raise their child or children without any physical-correctional contact the same way the author raised his children. The author also points out the possible repercussions that parents are subject to experience should they make physical contact with their child or children in an attempt to correct them. In spite of all this, the author wanted to validate to himself and others that people can raise their child or children without subjecting them to physical or verbal abuse and can train, educate, and direct their child or children to becoming productive, responsible, and functional individuals regardless of what they may decide to pursue in the way of their careers of choice.

Furthermore, the author figured out a way to make parenting simple by teaching and training his children while they were developing fetuses in their mother's womb and continuing after birth up until the age of 5 or 6 and beyond, which happens to be the most critical years of a child's life. Moreover, this early training and teaching method will make raising competent, capable, reasonable, and tolerant children one of the easiest processes that any parent could make themselves available of including making life enjoyable for themselves. Likewise, this early training being taught to your child or children will remain with them throughout their entire lifetime. Not only should your child or children excel in their self-esteem, self-respect, and abilities, but as a parent or parents you will not be raising a problem child or children like the author became in his early childhood and beyond that needs to be avoided at all costs. There are also several important safety subjects that a parent or parents of older children should know about that should be taught to their child or children by their parent or parents that are also discussed in this book as a means of assisting them with their parenting techniques.

Most of these techniques were created and developed by the author that include instructing a parent or parents on how to develop a positive child and how to correctly discipline a child's behavior according to the author's beliefs. There is a three part section on how to protect and safety train your child or children in addition to how to handle inappropriate sexual behavior. Furthermore, there are examples for teaching parents how to handle their child or children if and when they ever witness them exploring their bodies including their special private body parts. This parenting book also includes a chapter on how parents can teach their child or children in understanding and accepting responsibilities and a section on the realities of being a parent or parents. The initial concept of the author's training was designed by him in order to develop a means to control and correct any of his children's misbehavior activities without using any form of physical correctional methods that have been handed down from parental generations to generations in order to control and correct their child or children, and a whole lot more of relevant parental information, so let's get started.

CHAPTER 1

Congratulations

You're Gonna Have a Baby or Babies

The majority of people don't realize that they can start training their child while they are in the womb, but it is very easy to do and the results can be astronomical that you will discover when the time comes for the new arrival of your baby. For those of you who have already given birth, don't worry because you can still start very early training your babies with this same process, and the sooner you start the better your rewards will be. Nevertheless, this training process is only recommended before birth and up to 5 to 6 years of age depending on how fast your child is developing. However, once a child has reached 5 to 6 years of age their brains have already been conditioned and programed by their parents in a way that will, hopefully, still allow their brains to receive new input. Notwithstanding, after age 6 this process may be used, but it may take longer for your child to learn the ramifications of the training because their minds are developing at a faster rate than that of a new born.

The first thing both parents need to do is to agree on a simple noise, whistle, clapping your hands, snapping your fingers, or some other means to start communicating with your unborn child so as not to confuse the child once the child is born. The only main point here is that both parents must be in agreement as to the sound you will be training your child to react to since this sound will get your child's attention no matter how old they are or become as they will never forget this sound. Example: In my situation I chose snapping my thumb and middle fingers twice to make a clicking sound. Unfortunately, my wife at that time in my life didn't believe this training would accomplish anything, therefore, she refused to go along with my idea. Anyway, getting back to training the unborn child starting at approximately 3 months into her pregnancy and over time whenever I got the chance I would snap my fingers around my wife's belly. The neat part about this is that when the baby started kicking in the womb, I would snap my fingers and the kicking would immediately stop. When the kicking started again, I would just snap my fingers again and the kicking would stop again. I did this right up until it was almost time for her to deliver the child. For those of you who cannot snap your fingers, people can still buy a Cricket Clicker on Amazon that will be just as effective, especially, for mothers. When the child was delivered and was in the incubator, (this will be explained later) I snapped my fingers again and immediately my baby boy zeroed in on the sound confirming my theory about training a child while they are still in the womb. Likewise, it even gets better, as I found out the more time the child had to develop the faster he would zero in on the snapping sound. It was amazing to see the boy grow and never once did he forget that snapping sound.

    Three years later we had a baby girl and I used the same finger snapping sound to train her while she was still in the womb and when she was delivered, she reacted immediately to the snapping sound and zeroed in on the direction it was coming from. Now for the exciting part, as it turned out both of my kids would immediately stop whatever it was that they were doing and zero in on the snapping sound and react to whatever I was asking them to do. This process was amazing in that I never had to do anything other than snap my fingers to get their attention, and even to this day they both react to the sound of snapping fingers, and my boy or rather young man now at 41 and my daughter is 38, and neither one of them have forgotten that snapping sound.

Okay, let's look at some real life situations that started to happen around the time the kids were 1 and 3 years of age. Whenever these two would get into a tug-a-war with their toys or were fighting with each other, I would simply snap my fingers and immediately all activity would cease. Now all I had to do was point to a room or a chair and then pointed my finger at which kid I wanted to go to their room or to sit in a chair. Never did I have to raise my voice or even had to physically punish them (which I don't agree with anyway) and they always reacted accordingly. I remember having to go to the DMV in California with both kids and when we got inside the building, there were several little kids running around all over the place with their embarrassed parents trying to get control of these loud and incredibly obnoxious kids.

Due to the noise these kids were making it made it difficult to communicate, so I snapped my fingers and pointed to the two chairs I wanted my kids to sit in and then I got in line. For the next 45 minutes we waited while the other little monsters were running around screaming, and hollering, and totally uncontrollable by their parents. Nevertheless, my turn was finally over and when it was the time to leave, I simply turned around towards my two kids from across the room, snapped my fingers, and gave them a hand signal to come, and we left the DMV while all the women looked at us with their mouths hanging wide open in disbelief. They could not believe that my kids, or any kids for that matter, could behave that well in a public building as young as they were at that time.

In our opinion, it is vital that people have well-behaved babies and children and develop the ability to correct any given situation that your babies or children may become involved in regardless of their age. Whether it is snapping your fingers or developing certain sounds like a distinct whistling sound, clapping your hands, or whatever suits your needs and works for you to train your unborn baby; just start doing it at regular intervals as close to the wife's belly as you can. When the time comes, you will be glad you did because it will make parenting simple as it will relieve a lot of the stress that comes with parenting and raising obedient children.

Now for those of you who already have young babies or kids up to 6 years old, or older, you can simply train them in the same manner. However, in order to develop a sound your kid or kids will react to, just start experimenting making different sounds until your child or children zero in on your position. This will tell you the sound to use when you want the attention of your kids and want them to pay attention to you to receive your instructions or directions. Remember to be consistent and don't try to use other sounds once your babies or kids have learned to react to your specific sound. Also, please don't try to use your voice to attract their attention because as time goes by and depending on where you are at, your children may not be able to hear your voice, but they will zero in on and hear the distinct sound that you have trained your children to listen for.

It was funny at the time, but I vaguely remember thinking that these women and men were in dire need of a parenting guide book that would help them raise and control their children. However, it never crossed my mind to write such a book until some 52 years later because the babies and little kids today are even more misbehaved and obnoxious having no manners whatsoever, especially, in a restaurant setting. At our age, we have very little tolerance for loud, obnoxious, and misbehaved babies and kids as we did in our younger years. When we go to a restaurant, we go to eat and relax, but with yelling, screaming little banshies around, it makes our restaurant outing almost unbearable because parents do not know how to control their babies or kids. The last thing people want to hear or see at a restaurant is another person's kid or kids yelling, crying, running around, or making noises that irritates and interferes with their meal. People don't pay money at a restaurant just to hear other people's obnoxious kids yelling and screaming because it is rude, irritating, discourteous, ill-mannered, and disrespectful to all the other people in the restaurant. So, if you can't or don't know how to control your kids, people, don't take them with you to a restaurant, just leave them home with a babysitter or train them so you can control them in a public environment. The first time we took the kids out to a restaurant they were not much older than 8 or 9 months for the girl and about 3 years old for the boy. When we sat down at the table, it wasn't long before they started getting bored and antsy and then came the crying noise, so I snapped my fingers and the noise stopped for a short time only and then it started again. However, this time no matter how many times I snapped my fingers nothing happened, so we collected our two kids and went home since we do not like to irritate other people with misbehaved kids in a public setting. When we arrived home, I told both kids that they will never be able to go to a restaurant with us again as long as they cannot act like regular people. The next time we told the kids we were going to a restaurant they wanted to go with us, but we told them no to make them realize that I meant what I said to them the last time and we got them a babysitter. When we returned home, both kids approached us and stated that they would behave if we would take them with us the next time, and I told them we will see.

The next time we decided to go out again the kids again begged us to allow them to go with us and I told them that if they acted up in the restaurant, they would never go with us again until they were old enough to act like regular people and they agreed. So off we went to the restaurant and just as I figured, the kids were perfect in their behavior, and they even started pointing out to us the other parents whose kids were acting up yelling and being obnoxious. To make a long story short, we never did have anymore problems with our kids in public places even though they were very young. Likewise, we were always being complimented by other people on how well our kids behaved in public.

So the answer is, yes, people can start training their babies before birth and for a while after the children are born and up until about the age of 6 that will have the most lasting impact on your children. The sooner people start training their babies, the simpler parenting will be, and the sooner they will be able to enjoy their kid's company and be proud of them knowing that they will not be acting obnoxious when they are out in the public. Likewise, teaching your baby to read starting at birth and forward is also relatively easy for anyone to do. There are materials out in our society today that are called "How to Teach Your Baby to Read" and "Teach Your Baby Math" by Glenn Doman. This is a kit designed to give your baby a major head start in life in learning and developing your babies' brains that can place them way ahead of their peer groups, and not only is it fun to do, but it will also build a major bonding between you and your baby or babies.

CHAPTER 2

The Positive Child

In order to raise a positive child or children people will need to set priorities for their kids and a developmental process in order to realize the results people would like their child or children to achieve in order to eventually become functional and productive individuals in our today's society. This, as you might have guessed, is not an easy task to be taken lightly in a world where kids are bombarded with garbage that is constantly being placed in front of them via the Internet, indoctrinated with television garbage, and a myriad of other information that can and will tempt, attract, and try to get your kids attention. The majority of this garbage is just that, garbage, and it will deter your kid from becoming a positive person. What can a parent do that deals with Alcohol, Drugs, and eventually Sex or anything else vying for your kids attention? Good question, and that is why it is important to start training your babies early in order to give them a fighting chance in today's society.

My daughter recently had her first baby and for the first two years this little girl had very little exposure to TV, Internet, or news media that could distort her brain or learning process. Now at the age of 2 she has been assessed as being way beyond her age bracket in intelligence and communicates well with a peer group of kids that are 6 and 7 years old. Just recently my daughter's family decided they will be having a movie night on Saturdays only and allow their daughter to watch Disney movies as a family unit. They also allow her to watch only 30 minutes of cartoons a day and no more at this time in her little life. Likewise, this little girl is constantly involved with the family and at pre-school where she can interact with other kids her age and the older children because she can associate with them better on their level. By doing this her social skills are far more advanced of where a typical 2-year old would be functioning. When we were bringing up our daughter, she was constantly watching me (unbeknownst to me at the time) studying and complaining when I would get a grade of a "B" or less on whatever subject I was being graded on. This in turn motivated her to start reading more and more books, and by the time she was in the third grade she had read over fifty or sixty books. Her vocabulary was amazing and her ability to learn increased exponentially.

Nevertheless, we believe young children at an early age should be allowed and be able to develop on their own and be able to start making their own decisions regardless of how small the decisions are with proper supervision. The decision-making process will allow children to start to learn how to understand what is acceptable and what is not acceptable in their own little world. However, as parents you should be directly involved in your children's decision-making process by offering polite corrective instructions, so as not to discourage your child's thought making process, and be sure to answer all their questions. Also, it is perfectly okay if your children fail to make the right choices or decisions early on in their lives. As parents you can help them grow through this experience and assist them by instructing them how to learn from their mistakes. At this juncture I think an example is in order and this example is strictly a thought process of the author who raised and taught his kids starting in the womb before birth and after throughout their growing process to pre-adulthood, and constantly questioning his kids as to how they derived at their conclusions.

Example: The first thing I taught my children was to respond to the question of "What can you do?" and they were instructed to yell back "ANYTHING," thereby eliminating any negativity that might enter their little brains. We indicated that this response was a game so that the kids would enjoy and get a kick out of yelling "ANYTHING." For the next couple of years or so when the kids said that they couldn't do something we asked them to do, we simply asked them, 'What can you do?" and they started responding with (you guessed it) ANYTHING. Now remember, these two kids are only about 2-1/2 and 5-1/2 years old and both on the same intelligent level. Oh, yes, I forgot to mention that the boy is a brain-damaged handicap who was damaged by the doctor who delivered him because of the doctor's negligence and his lack of experience 41 years ago in my boy's situation at birth. Nevertheless, I treated both children exactly the same as they would not know for a few years that something was not right with one of them, but that's another book that the author will be writing at a later date.

Okay, getting back to where we were, now the kids at the age of about 2-1/2 and 5-1/2 really started enjoying this ANYTHING answering process and when they didn't say it loud enough, I simply responded with sorry, "I can't hear you," until they said ANYTHING loud enough to not only convince me, but it started convincing them that they had the ability to do anything. Even to this day, if I ask either one of them this question, they immediately respond with "I can do Anything" even at their current ages of 41 and 38. Moving on to phase two of learning how to develop a child's positive outlook, I began teaching them my thought process that goes something like this. Both children were taught to think about what they wanted to do, then weigh the good (positive) and the bad (negative) aspects of the situation they were thinking about and based on what they analyzed to come to their decision, be it right or wrong, and to stick by their decision no matter what the consequences turned out to be.

Granted it took several years for the my kids to grasp this thinking process, but by the time they were 8 and 11 years old, respectively, they both had this thought process locked into their brains. By the time both kids were 13 and 16 years of age this thought process was calculated in their brains instantaneously weighting both the pros and cons of their decision-making process, and 99 percent of the time their decisions were correct. Today, both my kids use this same thought process to process any situation they encounter no matter how difficult the situations may be. My boy is still with me to this day as I swore that I would take care of him for the rest of his or my life, whichever comes first, for he is my flesh and blood and as healthy as can be even though I had been told that he may not live past 5 years of age by some feckless doctors years ago. My daughter is doing fantastic at what she does best and both are very well-adjusted and conduct themselves with confidence and continue to grow in their self-esteem and self-confidence.

Another thing that is important, or at least it was to me, was to always make sure that my children learn to develop their self-respect, self-esteem, and learn to be courteous toward others. Even though this concept may seem to be an easy achievement it can take a long time in developing. However, if self-respect is incorporated in the beginning of the training process, the children will develop exponentially in their self-esteem. Therefore, it is vital that parents shower their children with praises when they do the right things, which in turn encourages them to develop into the person that all parents (we hope) would like to see their children eventually become when the time comes for them to join society. This entire learning process can begin while the child is in the mother's womb, but definitely at the time your child is born.

At this time parents may not realize the importance of this type of early baby training, but trust us when we tell you that it is more than worthwhile as you will learn as your children grow up. Whether parents use our training method or another method doesn't make much difference as long as parents start training their babies as soon as they can with all the love and kindness they have.

CHAPTER 3

The Endless Parent World

of Saying

No

This particular form of communication between parent and children has been going on since the beginning of time, and as parents you are well aware of the word No. Only this time it will become your turn to use this noun as a means to control your children, but the question becomes, is there a better way to control children without using the word No? The answer to this question is a definite YES. So, if parents don't want their child or children growing up with a negative attitude about life in general or end up having adverse behavioral and flare up problems, then parents need to learn a better way to get your point across to your children other than using the word No. We recommend parents view the internet on the word No and understand that kids hear the word No about 400 times a day according to a UCLA survey, and as much as 150,000 times as they are growing up. However, the last number is not anywhere near the correct number and after recalculating, the actual number is around 1 million times by the time children are 7 years old and over 2 million times of hearing the word No by the time they reach 18 years of age; this includes hearing the word No from other people.

Before we get started, parents need to understand and know that the human brain cannot comprehend or process a negative statement or command such as the word No right away like the word STOP can. Technically speaking, the brain has to stop and figure out what the concept of No is meant and for what purpose in order for the brain to comprehend and understand before the rest of the body can react to the command in order to cease an action. Likewise, there are several words and combinations of words that also convey the word No, such as "By no means, Under no circumstances, No way, Not on your life, Absolutely not," and several other combination phrases and exclamation words. Therefore, I will be explaining a few ways I raised my children so they would not become anything like me because of the way my brothers and I were raised, constantly being badgered and inundated with put down exclamations by our parents while using the word No.

It is important that parents learn to use alternatives to the word No as early in their child's developmental stages as they can. Children usually start recognizing certain words starting at around 5 to 6 months of age or sooner at which time their pattern of communication and comprehension is set in motion in the earliest days of their development. In other words, parents, without even realizing it, make or break their children's thought and understanding processes very early in their children's lives, which in turn means that by the time your child is ready to enter the adult world they will either be very positive and confident in their thought processes or they will be pessimistic, cynical, dismissive, and uninterested throughout their lives without even realizing what they are doing or why they are doing it. Furthermore, parents could end up having children that grow up to be adverse, harmful, detrimental, bad, rebellious, violent, and disadvantaged by the time they are ready to enter society which is not what any parent would desire for their children, in my opinion anyways.

Allow us to give parents an example: Using the word No vs. the word Stop! As we previously stated my son is a brain-injured child and has very little visual acuity along with having no depth perception. Notwithstanding, one day my wife was leaving our Real Estate Business and going over to our Real Estate Mortgage

Loan Business offices, which happens to have an extremely steep stair case, when our son managed to get ahead of her by about five feet or so and managed to reach this stair case before her, which he did not notice, and just before he started to take the next step my wife yelled out the word STOP, and fortunately, our son immediately stopped as he had been trained to do upon hearing this word. By using the word Stop as opposed to the word No his brain instantly recognized the word and prevented our son from falling down the stair case thereby preventing him from sustaining any injuries or, God forbid, possibly losing his life. In this situation had my wife yelled out the word No, our son's brain would have had to first process the word No. Then his brain would have to comprehend the meaning of the word No, within a matter of a split second, which would have been too late even for a normal person to comprehend let alone a brain-injured child and the end result could have been disastrous to say the least in this particular situation. Fortunately, everything turned out okay and life went on as usual that day. Incidentally, we only related this incident because my wife thought this scenario might be helpful to other parents or a parent in a possible crisis situation that might involve their child or children.

So what are parents to do? Learn a better way to deal with raising your children by not using the word No. How I did this goes something like this: When my kids started crawling and headed towards something that I did not want them to get involved with, for whatever reason I deemed inappropriate, I would simply snap my fingers twice, get their attention, and then redirect their attention to something else. As my kids grew older like 1 through 3 years of age I did a lot of finger snapping and redirecting my kids in addition to starting to explain why I did not want them to do a particular thing depending on what they were up to. Having trained both of my kids while they were in their mother's womb by snapping my fingers, made raising my kids not only enjoyable, but also one of the easiest and simplest things I ever had to do in my life was raising my children. There was no need for yelling, hollering, shouting, or even using the word No when my kids started to do something that I believed was wrong, or that I didn't want them to do or touch, I just simply snapped my fingers twice to get their attention and explained why I did not want my kids to do certain things.

The neat aspect about all of this was that after explaining to the kids why I did not want them to do certain things, my kids started learning to ask me questions as to why I didn't want them to do these certain things. This was great because my kids were now learning how to formulate their own thoughts and analyze this or that particular situation even though they may not have understood the complete reason why I asked them not to do a certain thing. Nevertheless, my kids were going from existing thinkers to now becoming abstract and imaginary thinkers and, eventually, my daughter became an out-of-the box thinker always seeking a better way to achieve whatever it was that she was doing instead of following the crowd, so to speak. I also taught my kids not only how to think out of the box, but also taught them that they were to think about any situation they were about to undertake and figure out how to make life easier for themselves when they undertook whatever it was they were going to do. Instructing my kids in this thinking process would not only make life easier for them, but their way of doing things would astound the majority of people, which they have done over and over again because of their abilities.

In view of the fact that the majority of parents were not raised by their parents to develop a different thought process that would lead the way for them to doing things differently, today's parents are the typical go along to get along parents. So, based on this scenario, how does one think the parents of today and in the years to come will attempt to raise their children? You're right, the same old thoughtless way by using the devastating word No. Parents need to understand that even before their child is born their minds can be trained, and after they are born parents are basically dealing with a blank computer mind and parents are the programers. Remember, a child developing in the womb will be experiencing everything the mother experiences and how the mother reacts to any given situation will be transmitted to the child by way of her physical and neurological system. In other words, if a mother is always obsessing about something, reacting to situations in anger, always doubtful, having trouble making decisions, feeling guilty, has been physically harmed or hurt during her pregnancy, her physical and neurological system will be transmitting her reactions to the baby.

This situation in turn will eventually have an affect on the child sometime in their future, and they will have no idea of how they managed to develop any of these previously mentioned characteristics. Essentially, this is what I would refer to as a metaphysical metamorphosis's transference. The question now becomes, will parents initiate good input or bad input? The answer can only be decided by the parents, which will eventually determine how their children will develop, progress, and how well they will navigate through life, or worse yet, your children end up being separated, divorced, incapable of having or maintaining a long term relationship, and the possibility of being incarcerated simply because they couldn't cope with or understand how they turned out the way they did. Fundamentally, all of these situations can be avoided or greatly reduced by kind, considerate, and loving parenting. The choice will only be left up to the parents, so make a wise decision, parents, for the benefit of your children and learn to eliminate the word No from your vocabulary and try to be positive parents.

There is one more thing I would like to point out to the parents before moving on and that is the same old propaganda that we have all heard at one time or another which is "It takes a village to raise a child." Parents, this is the most ridiculous statement that I have ever heard and I will explain why. Hardly anyone else has your child or children's best interests at hand or on their minds. Likewise, the way you decide to raise your children may be completely different from other people who might think that you should raise your children according to the way they think. Well, think again parents, because your children are your children and you don't need other people trying to raise your children in a different manner than what you have decided. If parents want their children to be around other people, that is just fine, as long as these other people can keep their hands off your kids and their mouths shut when it comes to the mental development of your children.

CHAPTER 4

The Positive Parents

VS.

The Negative Parents

It was suggested by my wife that I should say something concerning Positive Parents vs. Negative Parents. Unfortunately, we usually have only one set of parents, and therefore, I can only relate to the readers what I experienced as a child growing up with what I believe were negative parents. The way I came to this conclusion about my parents was based on how I raised my children, especially, when I got custody of both of my children. At that time my boy was almost 7 and my daughter was 5 years old when they came to live with me with their mother having visiting rights for a period of time. Eventually, I agreed to go along with a joint physical custody arrangement, but for no longer than a week at a time in the event that something should happen to the kids. Sadly, my ex-wife is a negative and pessimistic person and a week under that kind of influence is more than enough to derail the children's thought processes. Anyways, as a kid growing up I was the second oldest out of 4 boys, and for some unknown reason I was constantly beaten, yelled at, told that I would never amount to anything, was dumb and stupid, and just about everything and anything else in the way of negativity that my dad could think of to make life miserable for me.

Even though my other 3 brothers were treated badly at times, I seemed to get the brunt of the old man's punishment for reasons unknown to me even to this day and continued until I entered the military. Technically, I should have ended up in a mental institution, in total depression or in prison, but for some unknown reason I had the ability to think on my feet, and that may be what has saved my life all of these years. Life for me as early as I can remember was miserable and disastrous to say the least. Unfortunately, a little later on at about 10 years old I fell in with the wrong group of kids growing up and started getting into a lot of trouble to the point of being told that I would be sent to reform school if I didn't straighten out. Honestly, I didn't care, as I came to believe that no one cared about what happened to me. I had no self-respect, no encouragement, no self-esteem, and no respect for anyone else, so basically, I was on my own at a very early age. Since I was told that I was pretty much feckless I figured that I might as well get into trouble to get attention because no one seemed to care about me anyways or about what might happen to me.

Now, on the other side of the coin, let's look at the Positive Parents of which I consider I was, and how I raised my children. Back in 1967 I had an event take place that completely changed my thought process about kids because at the time I really hadn't ever thought about kids. Nevertheless, I was on patrol with a Korean White Horse platoon, also known as the Korean 9th infantry division, in Viet Nam when all of a sudden I hit the ground thinking that I had been shot in the lower right side of the stomach before I went unconscious. However, when I woke up, I was in a place called Cam Ranh Bay (pronounced Cam-ron Bay) where the military hospital was located and had been operated on and put into a recovery ward with the other GI's. When I became coherent, I was told how lucky I was because my appendix almost ruptured in the jungle in which case I would no longer be here, but somehow they managed to med-a-vac me by helicopter to the rear area and operated on me before my appendix ruptured.

Nonetheless, a few days later I was told to get up and walk around, which I did very slowly and bent over like a very old person. As I was walking I noticed a very large enclosed cage having a tin roof over the entire area that contained wounded prisoner enemies known as POW's who had been picked up in the field and brought to the hospital to be saved. Nevertheless, I noticed several 8, 9, thru 15 year olds that had been pretty much messed up from being shot or blown up with limbs missing, etc. However, I ran across a little 9-year old Vietcong who had got his hand mutilated by a shoebox bomb meant for some unlucky GI, but it blew up on the kid before he could use it on someone else. Again, to make a long story short, I made an agreement with God and asked him that if he would allow me to survive the war and I was fortunate enough to be allowed to be granted kids that I would prove that parents did not have to ever hit or abuse any child in order to raise good kids.

Well, I made it home, and a few years later I married, and remembering the request that I had asked God for and was granted two beautiful children, and now it was up to me to raise these two kids without ever using physical punishment to get them to mine me or do what I asked them to do. As I was starting to raise my two children I was fascinated with the way they viewed different things and how they reacted to them at their very early ages. I noticed that very young children at 6 or 7 months old are very curious of just about everything and have to explore, touch, mouth, and feel everything they come in contact with in their little world. In my opinion, this is the point that makes the difference of becoming a positive parent or a negative parent depending on how they react towards their child in any given situation. Therefore, parents should be calm and involve themselves with their kids encouraging them by calmly distracting their child in order to turn their attention to something else they would like their child to focus on. On the other side of the coin, we have the negative parents that will yell and holler at these innocent babies and even hit them in an attempt to get the child to stop doing whatever it was that got the parents' attention in the first place.

To give parents an example of how they should react and not use the word No, we will explain an incident that happened to my current wife many years ago. When my wife was a 3-year old, her Dad came back from fighting overseas in World War II and rejoined his family. He had also brought home with him his military revolver and put his loaded gun in a safe place, or so he thought. One morning the typical 3-year old was up earlier than her Mom and Dad and knowing where the gun was, she decided to play with it when her Mom and Dad came out of their bedroom. Immediately, her Dad started to shout "No" when her Mom stopped him and calmly said to their daughter, "Oh, come and see what I have for you over here," and the little 3-year old put the gun down and ran over to her Mom to see whatever it was if nothing else but a big hug. By not shouting the word "No," and scaring the little girl, who may have pulled the trigger by being frightened, and by redirecting the little girl's attention, her parents prevented a shooting that may have maimed, crippled, or killed someone in their family, and instead, by remaining calm, they saved a life in their family that day.

So now, the question is, "What have these two different parenting techniques accomplished?" The positive parents did not startle, condemn, scare or frighten their child, but very calmly redirected their child's attention thereby encouraging, building awareness, and instilling self-assurance in their child. Because of the negative parents' response and reaction, they not only startled, condemned, scared, and frightened their child, but they are also destroying the child's developmental, experimental, and curiosity abilities, and their brain thought processes, thereby stopping their child from progressing any further. Even though these parents may think they are loving parents, in reality, they are destroying the child's learning abilities at a very tender age. Children that experience these types of negative parents will be the kids that will go wrong, become followers, have depression, and have very little self-confidence and self-respect. In other words, negative parents, even though they think they are doing the right thing for their children have in fact condemned their children to mediocrity by condemning their children's self-worth. For those of you who do not think this is true, just look around at the young adults and how messed up the majority of them are in today's society.

The majority of these young people's parents were negative parents, even though no one could convince them of being that way, but because these kids were constantly being controlled, not being able to make their own decisions, and always being told what to do, and basically, not being allowed to think on their own, has greatly limited these kids ability to function when they enter society on their own. If parents do all the thinking for their kids and not allow them to do the thinking, the kids become incapable of thinking for themselves and will more than likely make very bad decisions when they eventually leave the comfort of their home. The positive parents will encourage their children to ask questions and then they will offer the kids alternatives thereby allowing the children to arrive at their own conclusions and making their decisions based on the positive feedback from their parent or parents. Granted that children need to have guidance and limits set for their development in order to protect your children and how they interact with others so as to instruct them and make them responsible for their behavior and actions. Likewise, children need to be taught that there will be consequences for inappropriate behavior, which we will discuss in another chapter on what I consider is appropriate parental disciplining. Positive parents basically become child counselors advising, directing, training, and leading the children in an incontrovertible direction with constructive definitive suggestions instead of prison guards always telling the children what to do, how to do it, when to do it, or where to do something.

In the last above paragraph scenarios all a parent needed to do is offer suggestions such as "I would like you to do this some time in the next 10 or 15 minutes" or whatever the parents think is necessary or required in a given time factor. The same would apply to "When to do something or where to do something," but "How to do something" will require back and forth communication allowing for the child to come up with a reasonable solution to the situation. Again, positive feedback and input suggestions will create self-confidence, self-esteem, self-worth, and create a desire for children to want to participate in almost every situation. Moreover, as your children grow older you will have instilled the confidence they will need to become conceptual thinkers with the proper positivity of their parent's guidance. By incorporating these positive parenting techniques your children will continue to advance, and as they advance in age they will eventually be able to start learning on their own in the real world that you as parents are preparing them for when the time comes for them to enter society. Likewise, as positive parents you will now be able to back off and allow your kids to make more and more of their own decisions and be these right or wrong, they will have to learn to live with the decisions they make. More importantly, as positive parents you will be able to offer your kids the prerogative of calling you at any time they encounter a difficult situation to assist them in navigating their way through their difficult circumstances according to your knowledge and experience and, yet, allowing them to draw their own conclusions.

Since this is a parenting guide book, we can't spend more time on this subject, but for those of you who may be interested there are several other parenting books that you can purchase in the market place. However, most of them are written by clinical people and require a lot of time to read and frankly, they are rather tedious, and that is why I am writing this parenting guide because it gets right to the point. As the reader has already discovered, this parenting guide book has not been written from a clinical point of view in that we do not tell people what they should or should not do concerning the way they decide to raise their own children. However, our goal is, and has been, to assist parents by offering them various alternatives to the old ways of raising children the same way from generation to generation without ever changing or seeking a better way to raise their children. Like anything else in this world of ours, nothing remains the same and everything is always being improved for the betterment of our society, and the same goes for improving the ways parents raise their children in today's home environment.

We are sure that the majority of people have heard the cliche "Out with the old and In with the new," and that is exactly what we are proposing for child rearing in our today's society and for many more generations to come. We are always looking for ways to improving the way children are being raised and should be raised in a loving, caring, and considerate home atmosphere by loving, caring, and considerate parents.

CHAPTER 5

Correcting Children's Behavior

OR

Disciplining Children's Behavior

Before we get started I just want to point out that I detest, despise, and abhor, and have an aversion to the word discipline as I consider the term to be outdated and unacceptable in today's child rearing environment. In my opinion, the word discipline invokes violence and even though it is used in the Bible, I have to disagree with the writers who wrote this abominable word over 2000 years ago in the Bible even though it was inspired by the Holy Spirit. Furthermore, over 2000 years ago they did not have schools and the kids were not educated like they are today and nor were their parents educated, therefore, the only way parents thought they could discipline their children was to physically beat the kids as that was the way they were taught years ago. This type of disciplining is ancient history and was written in the Old Testament as stated by God so the Israelites could control their offsprings according to God's direction. Nonetheless, people today are not, hopefully, living in the ancient history time factor that no longer exists in our current modern day society as there are no more existing Israelites from 2000 years ago that we know of in our current day and age.

The problem with the discipling process back then vs. today was that it only worked for a very short period of time, or until the kids grew up and left the family to be on their own or their parents passed away. People, we are in the Twenty-First Century and yet parents cling to a 2000-year-old disciplining process because almost every Pastor, Preacher, and Priest preaches this historic outdated doctrine of discipline at one time or another that is based mostly on verse 12:32 in the book of Deuteronomy where God states: "See that you do all I command you; do not add to it or take away from it." The Bible is replete with verses on discipline mentioned in 12 books of the Bible from Deuteronomy through Revelations, but we have based this book on disciplining our children on a couple of verses of the New Testament where Jesus explains a better way to deal with children. Verse-1: Colossians 3:21 that states: "Fathers do not provoke your children, lest they become discouraged," and the second verse states in Mathew 18:10 "Take heed that you despise not one of these little ones: for I say unto you, that in heaven their angels do always behold the face of my Father who is in heaven." Yes, parents, we recognize that there are many more great verses in the New Testament, but we will leave it up to you to investigate them if you so desire. In addition, the dictionary states: "Discipline means to train someone to follow the rules" and does not mention anything about physical harm.

Nevertheless, the author needed to relate to the readers that this is strictly his own personal opinion and he will be explaining why as this chapter progresses. He also believes that people are far more educated today than they were 2000 years ago and, therefore, they need to get that old outdated historical physical disciplining nonsense out of their heads and join the real modern world of today.

So, let's get started. As the reader already knows I do not believe in physically correcting children and nor should anyone else for that matter as it indicates to the author, anyways, a major lack of intelligence. In his opinion, again, if parents are not smart enough to outthink or outsmart their children, then they have no right or reason to have children. Unfortunately, most anyone can have children without being required to submitting themselves to a series of tests that would determine whether or not people are even capable and maintain the mental ability of having and raising children. This is one of the reasons that our society has so many violent kids in all cultures, mainly because they are poor and have very little education and, therefore, lash out at society simply because their parents are not qualified, nor capable, and have no idea of how to raise their children in a different manner because they were not exposed to a correct or proper parent-training process and have not learned the techniques we will be pointing out in this parenting guide handbook.

Before my kids were born, I took the initiative at attempting to start training them while they were still developing in their mother's womb. Back in the late seventies and early eighties almost everyone thought I was a lunatic and nuts to think that anyone could train an unborn while they were still in the womb, except for me, of course. Needless to say, I proved all of them wrong and ended up with some very wonderful children, kids, teenagers, and now successful grownups.

Essentially, there is no trick to raising babies, to kids, to teenagers, and to young competent adults other than simple reasoning. The way I looked at it was from my perspective in that since I did not like being beaten three times more than any one of my other three brothers when we were growing up, I figured based on simple logic that neither would my children enjoy being physically beaten for anything they did or might do wrong. Likewise, in today's society a parent or parents could be thrown in jail for physically striking any child should the child call the police on their parents reporting them for child abuse, or the children could be taken away from the parents pending an investigation concerning these allegations. So, all I had to do was figure out a way to correct my children when they did something wrong, without disciplining them with physical violence in any way, shape, or form. Now that the baby girl was born and the boy was 3 years old I figured that I had plenty of time to figure something out in the way of what I thought would be the proper correction method. However, as time went on and the kids started growing up, and we were all getting along as a family unit, and growing close together, I knew that it was just a matter of time before all good things would come to an end, and that all these good things would eventually disappear and the time for non-physical correction would soon begin.

It wasn't long before my kids got into a physical confrontation with each other over some toy possessions and I immediately snapped my fingers and the fighting stopped. I then questioned the kids to determine who was wrong and it turned out to be my daughter when the thought entered my brain, and I thought why not have the kids name their own correction or punishment? What a great idea, so I asked my daughter what she thought I should do to her for hitting her brother? My daughter was to sit in a chair and not move, unless it was to go to the bathroom, but to sit in the chair until she figured out what her punishment should be. Remember that she is only about 10 or 11 months old and she sat in that chair for over 3 hours trying to decide how I should punish her. Finally she spoke up and told me she should give her brother back his toy and that would be it. It was really hard for me to maintain my facial expressions and not laugh, but I was amazed at the simplicity of innocents. Nevertheless, I agreed with her, but told her that giving back the toy was not enough punishment because she struck her brother, so I told her that she was to spend the rest of the day in her room and that she could come out for dinner. I was shocked to learn that this technique worked far better than any physical disciplining could have ever accomplished. My daughter went to her room crying for about 10 to 15 minutes and then stopped and stayed in her room until dinner. When she joined the family for dinner, the first thing she did was apologize to her brother stating that she would never do to him what she did to him again, then apologized to me, and I said loudly, let's eat dinner and that was that. My daughter never did hit her brother ever again after that incident throughout his life while she lived with us that I heard or knew of anyways.

As time went on this technique not only worked extremely well, but I only had to use it 5 to 8 times with my daughter and only 3 times with my son while they were growing up. When my son acted up and did something that he wasn't supposed to do, I repeated the correction-questioning-process with him and his first response, after sitting in the chair for over an hour, was to say that he was sorry. So like my daughter he thought going to his room for an hour would be punishment enough, and like my daughter I told him that was not enough and that he was not to watch any videos for the rest of the day and to stay in his room until dinner. Taking videos away from a brain-injured handicapped child was the worst kind of punishment anyone could do to him because his life revolved around videos as they do even to this day. My son's life revolves around Disney and Bible videos. Everything he relates to and how he associates and interacts with other people, places, and things he has learned from his videos and not allowing him to see his videos is probably the worst thing anyone could do to him in his world.

Needless to say, this correction process worked far better than I could ever have anticipated and imagined, and all I had to do was listen to how the children thought they should be punished and then add a little more to their punishment idea, and that is how I raised my children from early on in life through adulthood never having had to lay a hand, belt, switch, paddle, or anything else people use to discipline their children on my children. Physical punishment does not accomplish anything because once it is over, what do you think the kid will do next time? If they are anything like me when I was growing up, they simply figured out what they did wrong to get caught and the next time they do the same exact thing over and over again and never get caught. Kids have amazing brain capabilities and if parents can't or don't find a better way to correct their kids, they will end up with violent, pugnacious, antagonistic, bellicose, non-thinking kids who will never be able to make a correct decision or be able to adjust to any situation to become productive society members. More than likely they will end up in a medical facility, a mental facility, a correctional facility, or on the streets of America as a homeless person having no place else to go simply because their parents had no understanding of how to raise their children adequately or properly without the use of physical disciplining.

PART 2

What to do When Things Really go Wrong

People need to know what they can do when they catch or hear of their kids doing something really wrong, especially, if parents can catch their kids in the act at an early age. This is an incident that took place at my daughter's school while she was in the third grade at about the age of 8 or 9 years old. To make a long story short, I was driving around in Dana Point, CA. calling on Real Estate offices, as I was a Loan Officer, when I drove by a vacant lot, I saw what looked like my daughter talking with another girl and the two of them seemed to be having a lot of fun and enjoying each others company. So I pulled over to the side of the road and parked and continued to watch these two girls having fun. However, the closer they got I noticed my daughter and the other girl eating out of large bags of candy that each of them had when I decided to call my daughter over to the car, taking her by complete surprise. When she got to the car, I asked her where she got the candy from and listened to the typical denial explanation process when I finally snapped my fingers and told her to tell me the truth. As it turned out my daughter's friend had stolen her teacher's wallet out of her purse at school and took the money and went on a candy buying spree. When I asked my daughter why she didn't go her own way and leave the other girl, she had nothing to say, but I could not allow this kind of behavior to go uncorrected. Therefore, I told my daughter to get into the car and I took her over to where the police hang out at the local 7-Eleven store. Fortunately, there was a cop parked there so I told my daughter to stay put and that I would be right back.

Arriving at the police car I knocked on his window and when he lowered the window, I explained to him what I had encountered with my daughter and asked if he would have a talk with her and he agreed. So I went back to my car and got my daughter and told her that the policeman wanted to talk to her and I put her into the backseat of the police car. As I was getting ready to go back to my car my daughter wanted to know where I was going and I responded with "Sorry, but I don't want to live with a criminal" and told the officer that he could take her to jail and keep her locked up if she was not willing to listen to me anymore, and I went back to my car. As I was walking away I could hear my daughter crying, yelling "Daddy come back" as I headed for my car and just kept going. About 15 minutes or so later the cop signaled for me to come back over to his car and told me (loudly) that if he thought that my daughter would not be associating with the other little girl again, that he was willing to let my daughter go home with me. Next, I said (loudly) that I needed to be sure that my daughter would not commit anymore criminal acts and that if he wasn't sure, he should just take her to jail. The officer assured me, as well as my crying daughter, that she would never do anything like that again, so I allowed her to come home with me based on her word.

Was this a good resolution for me to do to my daughter at the time? Yes, was it a little harsh? To me, no, because activity like this needs to be corrected immediately and if it requires harshness to scare the bejesus out of my daughter, then this was the right decision to be made to correct this situation. Like I mentioned earlier, I think on my feet and do it very fast and decided that my idea was the best solution according to my thought process of weighing the pro's and con's of the present situation and sticking by my split second analysis and decision that I taught my kids starting at a very early age. The point being made here is that we never did have or encounter another problem such as this for as long as my daughter was living at home or with her mother. Needless to say, my daughter started associating with the good students at school and became a straight "A" student all the way through college where she graduated from San Diego State University and never got involved with the wrong kids again. To say that I am a proud father would be an understatement when it comes to both of my kids. Each of their own personal achievements in life so far have been amazing and far more than I could have ever imagined or expected, and what I think and consider that every parent or parents would wish for their children.

Another thing that happened to me was when I was approached by my two children one day, when they were 10 and 13 years old, they asked me what a spanking was? When I asked them why they wanted to know, it was because they heard about someone at school that was given a spanking by their parents. Because I had never laid a hand on my children they had no idea of what a spanking was so I had to explain it to them. I told my kids that a spanking was something parents did to their kids because they did not know or learn a better way to correct or control their children. Well, apparently, my explanation wasn't good enough for my kids because they both asked me the same question again. This time I told both of my kids to turnaround and when they did, I lightly patted each one on their buttocks. Both of their reactions were something I did not expect because even though I barely touched my kids they both started crying in total disbelief and humiliation to think that anyone would do such a thing to their own children. Not only were both of my kids upset and humiliated, but they were also in total disbelief and embarrassed to think that anyone could do such a horrible physical atrocity to their own kids. Because my children were in total disbelief and upset I had to calm them down in order to explain to them that some parents spank their kids because they were never taught, told, read, or realized how much damage they are doing to their kids when they spanked them.

Not only were my brothers and I spanked, but spankings turned into physical beatings. I remember going to school looking like a little Frankenstein having so many black and blue marks on my body, but that was how we were raised back in those days in the fifties and sixties. In fact, we didn't even realize that there was another way for kids to be raised as we thought that all parents spanked and beat the bejesus out of their kids. I even remember being spanked while I was in the first grade, for what reason is anybody's guess, but I remember getting ready to take a bath when my mother walked in and screamed. The first thing that went through my mind was "Ut oh, what did I do wrong now?" Not knowing what my mother was looking at staring at my naked body on my back side, but she told me to come to her room after I had finished taking my bath. After my bath I went to her bedroom and she told me to take my clothes off and to lie face down on her bed. Since this never happened to me before, I didn't know what to expect when she began rubbing me from my shoulders, buttocks, and down to the back of my legs just above my knees. As it turned out, my older brother asked me if I knew what my backside looked like? And I said no, then he told me that our Dad had beat me so badly with a belt that almost all of my backside was solid black and blue. Come to find out my mother was rubbing me down with alcohol and then using some kind of lotion to heal my backside. To make a long story short again, my parents kept me out of school for a little over a week and I loved it because everyday I got a rubdown and could watch cartoons all day, which was great for me. However, it wasn't until years later that I realized that the only reason my parents kept me home in those days was to prevent anyone at the school from knowing that I had been severely abused by my Dad and he could have been put in jail, and I would have been taken out of the house along with my other three brothers in order to protect us from any further child abuse or possible death.

Needless to say, I think the readers can now understand not only why I wrote this parenting book, but, also, I believe people need to learn a better way to correct their children without physical punishment and instead know that there are better and different techniques that can be used to correct children and learning how to out smart and outthink their children. As parents might now realize there are better nonviolent ways to correct even the most difficult child or children if they are taught and trained properly in the early stages of their young lives.

Both of my parents have long ago passed away, but I didn't let the old man pass without knowing what I thought of him. Parents, children are a gift from God and not punching bags or anything else one can think of to hurt children. I have read several parenting books and as I said early on most of them are unvaried and repetitive because most of them are or may have been written by people who may or may not have had any children or they didn't at the time they wrote the Parenting books. Others are written by MD's, RN's, Psychologist, or Psychiatrist who have studied children from all sorts of backgrounds, but technically they can only relate to the reader what they think and, unfortunately, it is usually related from a clinical point of view even though they may have raised their own children.

This book on the other hand is strictly written from a person's own personal experiences who was able to overcome extreme child abuse, teacher abuse, and being isolated from social situations where he could have been greatly influenced while he was growing up. Instead he found other avenues in which to channel his frustrations and lack of education that he would not recommend for any child to grow up in this type of environment. In fact there were only two times he was able to escape his home and family environment; one was when he was thrown out of his home by his Mother when he was 5 or 6 years old, given a paper shopping bag filled with some of his things because he decided to take out his frustrations on one of his mother's new plastic bowls by cutting it into pieces with a very sharp knife after he had been beaten with a belt for not washing the dishes clean enough while standing on a step stool. So, he was happy to leave and took off down the street to one of his friends' homes. His friend had a nice fort in his back yard that he could stay in and it was great. He stayed there for three days having a blast and not knowing that his parents had called the police and reported him as being missing, which was not true because he was told to leave by his mother. Eventually, the police found him 3 days later, and his friend's parents didn't even know that he was living in their backyard. Not realizing it at the time, but his reasoning and survival abilities were amazing to say the least at such an early age. Now that we think about it, this is probably the age at which he started becoming independent in reasoning and thought, but this event was also the beginning that would lead him to having developmental problems that was being caused by the way his parents were raising him. The second, and final time he left home was back in 1966 when he was given a choice to go into the military or be put in jail by his parents. Knowing what he knows today there was no way that his parents could have placed him in jail, but, hey, he was just a kid with very limited education so what did he know? Anyways, the reason for this ultimatum was that he was getting older and was tired of being beaten by the old man's fist so he got a hunting knife and slept with it under his pillow. He had, had enough and if the old man tried to beat him again, he was going to put a stop to him even if it meant eliminating him from this world. Needless to say, he forgot to take the knife out from under his pillow one morning and his mother found it and told the old man, hence, the reason for the ultimatum, but he was never physically fist beaten or otherwise physically hurt ever again from that day on until he entered the military.

We believe all the readers are now getting the point that physical punishment will only leave physical and emotional scars, and the animosity kids will develop towards their parents will never disappear from their minds. The damage that is done the very first time a parent puts their hands on a child in the form of physical disciplining can have and cause irreparable mental damage, and there is nothing a parent can do to undo the damage they have caused. Sure parents might get their kids to mind, but for how long? Parents may think they are doing the right thing for their children, but in whose opinion? God creates and lends children to parents for a short period of time, so take care of them. Hitting or beating children will never accomplish anything except creating mistrust and aggravation that will play on your children's brains for years to come, and you could end up with a very disturbed child that may never have the ability to mentally overcome the humiliation, mental degradation, mortification, and a blow to one's developmental process that physical punishment can cause.

Parents must realize that having a child or children is not a lifetime undertaking because your influence will only last for 18 to 21 years or a little longer before your child or children are on their own in our society. Consequently, when your child or children venture into the world and how they will view the challenge, will depend solely on how you programed them while they were developing and under the conditions they grew up in. If your child or children view their growing up process as being unfair, unbalanced, unreasonable, mean, and insensitive, they will more than likely avoid, or have no desire, or want to maintain a family relationship with their parents. In this situation, parents will only be able to blame themselves for the mistakes they made with their child or children by not finding a better way in which to raise them other than from a physical punishment standpoint. All this because the parents were not able to outthink or outsmart their child or children and were unreasonable and overcritical raising them.

On the other hand, if a parent or parents raised their child or children being understanding, considerate, thoughtful, sensitive, and reasonable then more than likely their kids will want and desire to maintain a continual relationship once they have left their home environment. These kids will know that they can constantly call on their parents for years to come for any advice or directions they may require in the future for whatever reason. Additionally, these kids will want their own child or children to know their grandparents knowing that their kids will also be treated correctly which will be the ultimate compliment any grandparents could ask for during their lifetimes.

Parents need to realize that by physically hitting, beating or verbally harming a child or children they are accomplishing and causing the following: The first of which is instilling fear, terror, agitation, trepidation, anxiety, and then comes apprehension, nervousness, antipathy, nightmares, and neurosis along with many more negatives that can have major affects on a child or children's brain processes. In other words, parents, you are destroying and isolating any chances of your child or children be able to adequately function and compete in the adult world in society when they are no longer under your control. Once any of these situations occur or develop in any child or children, the possibility of them functioning correctly or properly will be slim to none. These will be the kids who will grow up to become the people who will need some sort of psychological or psychiatric counseling assistance at one point or another in their lives thanks to the way their parents raised them.

Parents, the key word you should be considering is guidance when dealing with your child or children that will lead you towards instructions, directions, information, suggestions and nonviolent supervision that will enhance your child or children's self-respect, self-esteem, and self-confidence. By instilling these characteristics in your child or children their idiosyncrasies will lead them towards the attributes of having politeness, civility, and courtesy towards other people thereby developing admiration, esteem, and maintaining a high opinion of themselves. This in turn should allow your child or children to break down and negate any barriers that they may encounter when they enter the adult world when the time comes for them to enter society and not be burdened with developmental problems.

CHAPTER 6

Children's Safety Training

A

Priority

It is rather fascinating to watch people with their children when they are out in the public. When the children are still babies, they are fairly protected by their parents until the kids reach the age of 2 or 3. Granted parents will occasionally glance over at their kids to see what they are doing, then they shortly lose their attention. Parents may be talking with a friend, playing with their phone, which has become an addiction, or they are doing something or anything else, but paying attention to their kids. In this Chapter, I will relate to the reader how I trained my two children starting at the ages of 3 and 6 years old, but first I will give the parents the reasons that I did this type of training along with the benefits that will stay with your children all throughout their lives and, hopefully, they will pass this training onto their children in order to keep them safe.

A lot of parents will not like what I am about to relate to them, but the reality is that these Malum In Se, Lat. for evil in itself or naturally evil situations, can and do happen to children simply because all children are innocent, naive, trusting, and lack the ability to discern different situations and basically oblivious to the world around them. For this reason, children become prey and fair game for perverts, pedophiles, child molesters, and some of these perverts are usually a member of your family or extended families, your best friends, neighbors, Catholic Priests and other Church denominational clergy or even your very own spouse. Sure, there are a lot more of these kinds of people circulating all around, especially, those on the lookout for kids for organizations that traffic in child pornography and the child sex trade. However, these incidents are not limited to just young kids and if the readers watch the news or the internet, there are always articles of missing teens and people in their early twenties and older who are constantly going missing, or are being killed, buried, or thrown away, and being found years later. This does not even include the serial killers who are on the loose in our society today.

PART 2

TRAINING

Observance and Password

These areas of training are very easy for children to learn as I just turned the training into a game and the kids really enjoyed it and learned very quickly. Both the observance and password training is teaching the kids to learn how to observe their immediate and distant areas looking for anything suspicious or unusual in the way of people, cars, or anything that seemed to be out of place in their environment. The password was to be unique to the kids and one that all of us would learn to know and be ready to use if and when it was ever needed.

To start the observance training I drove the kids to a small grocery store and we parked in the parking lot where everything was easily observed. Next, I asked the kids to look over the area and to tell me if they saw anyone just sitting in their cars, trucks, or vans. In a matter of minutes both kids were telling me which vehicles had people in them. Next I asked them to tell me what they thought the people were doing like getting ready to start their vehicles, reading a book, on the phone, or just looking around like we were. We played this game for about 15 minutes and then left the small store area. It only took about 3 days before we had moved up to large parking areas around malls, schools, very large independent store areas, and other similar places. My kids started to become extremely aware of their surroundings while they were in any public areas.

The next process was to do the same observation, but we would be in the malls and other places with other people walking around and basically doing the same type of surveillance. However, this time the kids were to pick out people who did not seem interested in any shopping and who might be observing other people or kids. This surveillance process turned out to be rather interesting based on what my kids thought people or kids were doing and we, therefore, ended up having great conversations concerning this endeavor. Nevertheless, my children were learning the first phase of observance and they continue to do so even to this day. Unfortunately, I ended up having to do this observation process for my son because his visual acuity was not as it should be, but his hearing is incredible.

The password part of my training, as I mentioned earlier, was to be unique to the kids and one that all of us would learn to know and be ready to use if and when needed. To start this training the kids had to agree on a password that both of them understood and that would not likely be known by anyone else, even by accident, or anyone being able to come up with this password. Back in those days both kids chose the word "elbow" as their password although this was not our real password. Next, the kids were to pretend that I was a stranger and when I started to approach them, they were to ask for the password. If my kids did not get the right password, they were to turn and run yelling FIRE, FIRE, FIRE as loud as they could until someone came to investigate or find out where the fire was. Technically, parents can use any word or words they want, but the idea is to have your children attract as much attention as possible so that other people will come to their aid or find out what all the fuss and commotion is all about.

The reason I would not let the kids use passwords like HELP or PLEASE HELP ME or similar words, is due to the fact that people will ignore these pleads for help because they are afraid, or they do not want to get into trouble and may become the next victim of whatever is going on at that moment. Likewise, people do not want to get involved that may require them to speak to the police or have to become a witness at someone's trial. This is why I chose the word FIRE for the kids as it will attract just about anyone, if nothing else, out of curiosity. Another reason was that years ago in New York (may be some of you remember) a woman was being attacked by a guy with a knife in the middle of the night right outside her apartment complex at about 12:30 A.M. and she kept yelling for someone to help her, yelling that she was being stabbed, and no one in her entire complex was willing to come to her aid, and she died on the steps of her complex. So, the reader can now understand why they should pick a word that kids can yell to attract as much attention as they can if they have to run away from an attacker.

Both the observance and password training was just the beginning of my kids training and over time both kids started developing their awareness skills to a point that my sagacity abilities to instantaneously assess people started to rub off on my kids. As my kids sagacity abilities advanced so did their abilities at discernment and their analytical abilities which did nothing more than strengthen their awareness of their surroundings in which they may find themselves. As my kids got older and older, I became less and less concerned that something bad might happen to them because they have been taught the basics of survival tactics. Most of my training was learned in the war situation in Viet Nam and it just may be the reason that I was able to return home here in the United States.

PART 3

Reinforcing Awareness

There is not much to this procedure other than to see to it that my kids continued to practice and learn from their encounters and real life situations that they may develop or that they are exposed to at any given time. Likewise, as time went on I would point out different little things that my daughter should be made aware of so that she could avoid any possible snatch and grab situation that she could become involved in as a female. Unfortunately, young girls under the age of 21 are prime targets for all perverts, child molesters, and, especially, child pornographers, and the sex trade criminals who are always on the lookout for young girls and boys. There may be some ways in which girls can try and avoid these situations, but there are no guarantees. For example, let's say girls want to go jogging and decide to wear short shorts and skimpy tops outlining their body attributes, so to speak, they immediately become a target for a snatch and grab attack. Granted something may not happen for a while, but we can guarantee the girls that people are watching and sooner or later they are going to be approached or confronted. What happens to the girls at this juncture will depend on the intentions of the person they attracted. Even though nothing may happen at that moment, it is very likely that they will be followed by some pervert to determine what would be a better place to attack them. On the other hand, girls who wear regular shorts jogging with other people and not advertising their body attributes will not be inclined to attract too much attention.

To give parents an example of a real life snatch and grab attempt, my wife's daughter, who was a 14-year-old Freshman in High School, was walking home from school, only about two or three blocks from her home, when the daughter noticed a white van and a man supposedly mowing the grass between the curb and the sidewalk. As she was walking by the white van, she turned slightly as she noticed some movement near her when she saw the man was making an attempt at grabbing her, so she immediately ran away as fast as she could home. Once inside, she told her mom what had just happened, and her mom called the police who came right over, and they told the police what had happened, and where the house was along with where the white van had been parked. When the police went to the house where the van had been parked, they discovered that this event may have been a snatch and grab attempt. When the police spoke with the elderly lady who owned the house, she indicated that she did not have a gardener and that she was not aware someone was mowing her lawn. So, the police department, put police all around the area including surrounding the High School in the hope of catching the attempted kidnapper. Unfortunately, the mother never did hear whether this person was ever caught, but her daughter was safe and very lucky only because she had turned slightly and noticed this man before he could snatch and grab her.

Parents, being able to notice the little things can and will save a kid's life, like which way are curb-parked-vehicles' tires pointing. Are the tires pointing towards the curb, or are they straight ahead, or are they pointed out towards the roadway? Vehicle tires pointed toward a curb or straight ahead are not likely to be able to maneuver very well or fast enough, but a vehicle with the tires pointed out towards the roadway could be a sign of a snatch and grab, especially, if someone is in the vehicle seemly doing nothing and a young girl happens to walk by, she could be pulled or pushed into a vehicle, especially, a van, in a matter of seconds and the vehicle is gone just that fast. If the girl is pushed into a vehicle, this simply means that this is a two-or-more-person snatch and grab and the girl was not taught to observe her surroundings, thereby not noticing the other person or person's standing around or leaning up against a building. Parents, I can't stress enough why observance and awareness training can be vital for your children's wellbeing and safety, especially, if they are girls.

Nonetheless, constant practice will instill confidence in your children and make them far more aware and alert when they are out someplace on their own or with someone in any public setting. All throughout grade school, junior high, and high school I was always pointing out situations where my kids could be snatched and grabbed, at which point a parent may never see their child or children again, The bad part about this is that parents I have spoken with never think that this would or could ever happen to their kids, and some of them learn the hard way. Currently, the statistics indicate that between 2 to 3 million kids around the world get taken and go missing every year and 98% of them are young girls and teenager girls. So, our advice to parents is to reinforce awareness training in your children until it becomes second nature for them to be observant in whatever surroundings they may find themselves, whether by themselves, or with other friends, or people. Furthermore, be sure to practice the password with your children, including having different people you know approach your children offering them candy or suggesting they get into their car because their parents supposedly told this person to pick your kids up. Make sure the kids ask for a password and if it is wrong, make sure they turn and run yelling as loudly as they can FIRE, FIRE, FIRE until they get someone's attention. Should the person who was trying to snatch and grab your kids attempts to tell the person who came to the kids aid that it is all right because they are friends of the kid's family or are familiar with their family, instruct your kids to tell the person who came to their aid to call the police and take them to a store or somewhere safe where other people are and wait there until the police arrive to verify who this person is, who is trying to get the kid or kids, is really the person they say they are.

We are not trying to tell people to teach their child or children to be discourteous towards other people or strangers, but rather to teach them to be extremely aware of their surroundings and the people that may be showing an interest in them that may not be proper. To put this another way, is the person approaching your child or children being overly too polite, pretending to be like a father or mother figure, or even a grandfather or grandmother figure, who just may have the wrong intentions on their minds towards your child or children? Parents, we have all heard the other cliche that I taught my kids that states "Don't talk to strangers" and, yet, I always hear parents telling their kids to say hello to an unknown person for some unknown reason. To give parents another example: My wife, son, and I were leaving a restaurant and I stopped by a table having two young women and a little girl sitting there having breakfast to compliment the mother on how well-behaved her little girl was. After the mother thanked me for the compliment she turn towards her daughter and told her to introduce herself and say thank you and I immediately told the mother that her little girl should not be told to talk to strangers no matter how polite or kind they are and then we left.

The point of the aforementioned being made to parents is that, had the little girl been able to tell me her name, and if I had been a pervert, child molester, child pornographer, or a sex trade criminal, this little girl would now be an easy target because I would now have her name and sense she now knows me because of her mother who told her it was all right to talk to me in the restaurant it would now be a simple matter to get this little girl into a vehicle and disappear with her never to be heard from again. Therefore parents, do not let your child or children talk to strangers and, definitely, do not let them give a stranger their name under any circumstances when they are not in your presence where you could exert control over the situation.

CHAPTER 7

The Family Betrayal by Close Trusted Family Members and Friends

The next subject I want to talk about concerns the people parents think they can trust with their children. This includes members of your family or extended families, your best friends, neighbors, Catholic Priests and other Church Pastors or even your very own spouse. Did you know that over 90% of all child molestations begin with family members, spouses, your best friends, neighbors and even by Priests or Pastors? Sad, but nevertheless true.

The first things parents have to learn to do is restrict the handling of your children by all people who are not immediate family members and even this may not stop the molestation if your spouse is not the children's original father. To give the reader another example: A friend of ours was married to her second husband for 13 years when her two daughters started being molested by her husband when they were about 14 and 15 years old. Apparently, this guy's intentions was to eventually bed each of these young girls if he could persuade them to lie down with him. Fortunately, bedding these girls never happened or as far as our friend knew, but neither one of them said anything about what this guy did to them. When the girls were asked why they never said anything, they responded by telling their mother that they were afraid that by saying something they would breakup their mother's marriage to this person who was nothing more than a perverted molester, in our opinion. Nevertheless, our friend sat this guy down and told him that he needed to get help if he wanted to stay married. He apparently refused to seek help, and that was the end of her marriage to this guy because he couldn't keep his hands off of these two beautiful developing girls.

Parents also have to become aware of extended family members and their best friends. Because these people are not immediate family members, like Aunts and Uncles or Grandparents, the parents best friends and close acquaintances may not feel that they have to stay away from your children. A little touching, a little kissing, a little fondling, etc., by these people tells your children that these people are okay, so they think a little hug, a little kiss on the cheek, and picking up your children to hold them and touching them is okay; so, what's wrong with this kind of affection? Think about it, as parents you have basically told your children that this is appropriate behavior with these people because they are your trusted friends and they can't possibly have inappropriate thoughts running through their heads concerning your children. Time to wake up parents and face reality because these are the people that are being convicted of sex crimes every day in our society involving kids like your own children.

For those parents who may not believe this could happen to your children, then we suggest that all parents get on the internet and search "Megan's Law" or view "Criminal Watch Dog" in your immediate area and view all the Sex Offenders who have been released from jail that may be living in your area even as close as one of your next door neighbors. These are criminals who have been convicted of sex offenses and are registered Sex Offenders in your state and they are in all surrounding areas. Trust us when we tell parents that when you see these people walking around, they look like everyone else, just like ordinary people, but they are classified as sex offenders. Parents, this can be anyone you know or associate with and you may not even know it. This reasoning also applies to your local Priests or Pastors as children are told and taught that these are people who should be respected and looked up to, when in fact, they are some of the most dangerous pedophiles masquerading around as Holy people and, yet, they are the worst kind of child molesters. The bad part about all of this is that these Priests and Pastors do not or seldom get convicted of being pedophiles and are usually forced to resign instead of being prosecuted. This is a joke as these Priests and Pastors are in fact criminals and they need to be punished and put in prison just like any other perverts that prey on children.

To give the reader another example: Our family was invited to attend a church by a seemly nice lady while we were waiting for our car at the mechanics. This church was supposed to be full of nice people according to the lady we had spoken to, so we decided to give it a try on the coming Sunday. When we arrived at the church, the parking lot was full, so we parked out in the street and went into the church. Granted this church seemed to be full of nice people, a little too nice for my liking, but friendly nevertheless. Finding some seats for the three of us, we noticed two little girls in front of us with their mother who seemed to be occupied with something else other than watching her two little girls. Nevertheless, a few minutes later some guy who seemed to be greeting people, looked to be in his late twenties or early thirties, went over and greeted the mother of the two little girls and then he reached down to pick up one of the little girls and as he did he put his hand under her skirt between the little girls legs and lifted her up while he supported the little girl on his forearm that was now up against her vagina. This sick pervert was molesting this little girl by feeling her up right in front of her mother and the mother didn't even realize what he was doing to her daughter. The incident looked innocent enough, but this little girl was being molested right under the mother's nose. When this guy turned to attempt to give my wife a hug, she said no, and I told the guy that if he tried to hug my wife again that I would take his hands away from him and put him down. Needless to say, he left and so did we.

Parents, situations like this can and do happen everywhere everyday and it is your job and responsibility to see to it that your children are protected from these perverted people. The point being made here is not to let the people you think you know touch or physically handle and fondle your children unless they are within your presence or viewing area where you can react immediately to correct any situation that you, as parents, deem inappropriate behavior with your children. It is vital that parents do whatever is necessary to protect your children in any situation that may arise when your children are with you or around you when other people are around you, too. Parents, your kids can go missing and disappear in a split second even if you just look the other way for a second in order to answer a question or try to talk to someone who is with you. Things parents must understand is that child molesters, child pornography, and the child sex trade criminals are trained to observe parents and their interactions with their children and when they see an opportunity, they will act upon it immediately as that is their job. Trust me on this one when I tell parents that no child is safe because these people are always on the prowl.

This scenario also applies to parents' trusted family members and best friends who may not be having healthy thoughts about your children. These people are the perfect people for child criminals to get to know in order to learn about you and your children's habits in order to take advantage of either getting to know your children, or how, or when, to take your children. It is my recommendation for parents that find themselves involved in this kind of situation to make sure that your best friends new friend being introduced to you receives limited information concerning your children and make sure they stay away from your children until you as a parent can get to know them better even though that may not tell you much about any one particular individual. Therefore, it is advisable for parents to caution on the safe side as opposed to losing a child.

Parents, by constantly communicating with your child or children and asking them questions concerning how they were treated by your best friends or friends, or if they were ever handled or touched by your best friend or friends on areas of their bodies that no one should touch them, or lift them up in an inappropriate manner, as was mentioned in the previous church incident, then you can remedy and correct the situation immediately. Be sure to reassure your child or children that by telling you the truth that nothing will happen to them in the event that one of your best friends or friends attempts to become too friendly with your child or any one of your children. Nevertheless, caution is required here because children tend to want to remain in the good graces of their parents and they just might make something up in order to maintain that relationship.

So, caution on the safe side and don't approach your best friend or friends questioning them from an aggressive point of view. Instead, watch them with your child the next time they are together and see if there may be truth to what your child has told you. Does your best friend or friends interact appropriately with your child or are they doing things that as parents you might think to be inappropriate with your child? If it turns out to be true, then you can take the appropriate action by ending the relationship with your best friend or friends involved. On the other hand, if it turns out to be a misunderstanding and a possible exaggeration on behalf of your child, then no harm, no foul, and your relationship with your best friend or friends can continue. Nonetheless, always give your child the courtesy they deserve and investigate the situation yourselves in order to get to the bottom of any possible developing problem and under no circumstances should parents dismiss anything their child relates to them.

In situations like this, always give your child the benefit of the doubt, and if it turns out to be true, then reward your child and reinforce their correct behavior. In a similar manner, if your child was exaggerating or fabricating a story in order to gain your favor, be sure to discuss the situation with them and advise them on the appropriate way they should have responded. Nevertheless, encourage them to always tell you if someone may be doing something inappropriate to them, so that they will always maintain their confidence in their parents to turn to for help. Parents, in the event that the incident is in fact a molestation by someone you know, don't hesitate to call the police to handle this situation rather than you or your wife going to jail for trying to resolve the problem by yourself or yourselves.

CHAPTER 8

Inappropriate Sexual Behavior

We know this will or can never happen to our kids, really? Think back to when you were kids and your hormones were going on a rampage. Do you honestly think this will never happen to your children when they reach adolescence? Then think again. Please don't take this the wrong way because we are not saying that there is any appropriate sexual behavior in kids adolescence years, but human nature dictates that your kids will start experimenting with sexual activity when they reach their adolescent years around 13 or a little younger. The longer kids wait, the stronger the urge or desire becomes to indulge in sexual activity behavior, which is just a normal reaction to their hormones that are going wild. The only bad part about this event is that girls mature a lot faster than boys do and, therefore, they are inclined to want to experience what sex is all about sooner than boys; hence, the reason for so many abortions taking place all around the world.

Now parents may be asking what is causing this kind of desire of sexual behavior activity? As a parent, you are the main contributor to this behavior, and this is why. As you now know, children learn at a very early age even though they may not know what certain events are, or understand the full meaning of what is going on, or what the meaning of what the parents are doing, nevertheless, children are still recording these events in their developing brains. Things like watching their parents hugging, kissing, touching, or observing a few pats or gently grabbing or rubbing of each other's backside as a means of affection, but nonetheless, the children are learning, and their brains are recording, and storing this information that they will use later in their developing physical and mental lives. Please don't take this the wrong way parents as this activity between two people in love is perfectly normal and heathy for any relationship; all we are doing is pointing out to you that your children are also learning about healthy relationships between members in their immediate family environment through observation.

The problem with this process is that the parents may be the last to realize that their kids have become sexually active. The only thing parents can hope for is making sure they communicate with their kids and only hope they will delay their curiosity until they fully understand the ramifications that can occur should they get sexually involved with another person. Unfortunately, the majority of parents try to scare their kids by telling them about STD's, Gonorrhea, Syphilis, or other sexual diseases like Aids that they could contract should they interact with another person. However, this tactic can cause more mental distress, depression, and harm to your children, and it will more than likely have no affect at all on them as kids will be kids. The best a parent or parents can hope for is to educate your kids in inappropriate sexual behavior, and even catch them in the very early stages of their sexual activity, and then attempt to explain the pros and con's of sexual encounters to them at that time.

Let's look at an example I encountered with my daughter when she was in her Freshman year in High School, making her 14 or 15 years old. My daughter would invite girls and boys over to our place where they would go into her room, close the door, and do whatever young adolescent kids do. Because I had complete trust in my daughter seldom did I ever bother her while she was in her room studying or entertaining her friends. However, one day she came in and informed me that she invited a boy from school over to assist her in her studies and I didn't question her because she was a great student, which meant that this guy had to be a fairly smart person in order for my daughter to associate with him, or so I thought. Parents can be pretty oblivious and ignorant at times, and it never dawned on me at the time that my daughter's hormones may be going wacko and that she was developing faster than I could have ever imagined.

When the boy arrived, he seemed like a very nice and friendly person and even looked like he was rather intelligent, whatever that means, and I called to my daughter to let her know that her friend from school had arrived. My daughter came out of her room and greeted the boy, introduced him to me, and they both disappeared back into her room to study and she closed her door like she has always done, and I thought nothing about it like I have always done. I could hear them in her room through her thin door because they were asking questions of each other that gave me the impression that they were studying, which they were, but in a short period of time I would eventually find out that they were studying each other. As long as I could hear them in my daughter's room, I never thought much about what was going on between the two of them when all of a sudden I stopped hearing them talking to each other. This immediately caught my attention so I went to investigate and when I opened my daughter's bedroom door, I noticed that each of them were feeling each other's private areas with their feet while they were fully clothed except for their shoes. My first reaction was to beat the heck out of the boy, but my mind was already in full gear analyzing the pro's and con's of this situation and in a matter of a split second I had made my decision and calmly stated to my daughter that she was to tell the boy to go home or to wherever he wanted to go, but he had to leave.

PART 2

Understanding With Correction

AND

Explanation

Now, as a parent, it was my turn, but I should warn parents reading this book that how you handle this kind of sexual behavior will and can have a major affect that can cause a delay in your child's sexual activity, or more than likely it will cause a defiant attitude in your child that tells them in their mind, "Okay I'll show you," depending on whether or not you are a "Hell and Damnation" type of parent or a "Calm and Understanding" parent that can be a correctional parent presenting an immediate explanation that would make sense to your child that will make or cause them to think about what they were doing. My immediate reaction was that of being a hell and damnation parent with all my anger directed at the boy, but because of my ability to think analytically, my thought process started weighing the pro's and con's of this situation and knowing that it takes two to tango, I immediately came up with the following explanation to my daughter. In so many words, I told her that she could have any boy she so desired and all she had to do was to take her pants off, lay down, and spread her legs. However, I told her to think for a moment and decide if she wanted a boy because he wanted her body or did she want a boy who would be more interested in what she had up stairs in her head? Furthermore, I explained to her that boys at her age and older were only interested in her body and having sex, and if that is what she wanted, then she should make sure that she was protected and that the boys use the proper protection as well. On the other hand, if she wanted a boy or boys to respect her, her mind, and thought process along with her abilities to do just about anything she wanted, then she should think about it for a while and then make an informed decision, then I left her alone in her room.

As far as I know my daughter remained a virgin all the way through college and how far after that remains her business and no one else's. As far as my son is concerned, I attempted to have him watch a stripper with me once because it was a birthday party for one of the guys at work so I could see his reactions only to find out that he had no interest whatsoever. There is a big difference between what people determine to be normal children and those who have been brain damaged and are handicapped children. This was kinda disappointing to me at the time because every dad expects to share with their sons and I never did realize that my son would be different, but this subject will be in my next book.

PART 3

Break Time

A Little About My Wife

I pointed out to my daughter that I married my second wife because of her brains and her ability to think some 28 years ago or so because I don't remember how long we have been married and told my wife that if I remember how long we have been married, then it is time to trade her in for another wife. Since neither one of us pay any attention to anniversaries, not only have we saved a lot of money, but it has turned out to be great. Nevertheless, I first met her because she had sat on an open house when one of my client's kids walked into the home and decided to buy the house. However, my client did not want to deal with anyone but me concerning financing his son's home and instructed me to go tell this real estate person that I would be doing the real estate financial transaction for his son, as well as, my client. In response, I had to tell my client that it would be a breach of real estate ethics if I were to intervene in this real estate agent's business and that he would have to say something to her on his own. No problem, since this client of mine was part old school Samurai from Japan even in today's society he would get his own way one way or another. To shorten this explanation up a little bit, my client walked into this real estate office and took my business card and slammed it down on her desk and in a very loud voice stated "Mark Son" will be his son's Loan Officer or no deal. For the reader to get the full impact of this situation, this real estate office was located in Laguna Niguel on Pacific Coast Hwy right across the street from the Ritz Carlton located in a very wealthy area of Laguna Niguel, California. To say the least, all of those real estate agents that were in the office were terrified by this Japanese man and thought he might come back with a katana sword and cut their heads-off, but instead, my client went home and that was how I ended up meeting my current wife.

When I went to the real estate office to meet this person, and we finally met, what attracted me to her was when I was quoting all kinds of numbers and fractions to her, she showed no reaction whatsoever, and this was very unusual for a female real estate agent as the majority of them would get frustrated because they didn't understand mathematics very well. Next, they would tell me to go and do whatever was best for their clients, but not this one, and I figured either she knew what I was talking about or she was a great poker player. Anyways, we hit it off and, eventually, I discovered that she worked for Hughes Aircraft in their Black Ops Division developing a new radar system for the military; then I realized that she must have gotten a kick out of listening to me spouting out numbers and fractions to her that she was more than familiar with in her job. Both of us ended up doing business with my clients with her selling my clients' home in Newport Beach and selling my client two more homes in Laguna Niguel, one for himself and one for his son, and I did the financing on both homes. Afterwards, my client invited both of us out to celebrate at a very exclusive restaurant and we all had a great time together. The real estate agent and I became very close friends and I ended up sitting on open houses with her and doing all of her clients' mortgage financing and two months later we got married. Yes, it was fast, but my sagacity told me she was the right person for me, even as naive and gullible as she was, but I could rectify that over time. Thus far, it has been a great match and I've decided to keep her around a little longer. Plus, she is my editor and proofreader for all my books. However, enough about our life, so let's get back to learning how to deal with your kids.

PART 2

Continued

Parents, you need to understand that your kids are going to have sexual desires once they reach adolescence and they will have sex usually without your knowledge, just like you did when you were an adolescent. Therefore, the sooner you face this known fact, the sooner you will be able to deal with the situation in an appropriate manner. Kids will experiment and experience different sexual situations and as parents it is your responsibility to suggest and advise your kids when they reach this point in their lives. Communicating with your kids about what the pro's and con's of having sex are, will go a long ways towards making kids start to think about what they are being told. However, it is vital that you as parents don't try to defer this subject or try to scare your kids because they will eventually find out for themselves. Furthermore, parents should not rely on the school system to instruct your child or children concerning sexual matters because they are all taught how penises and vaginas function and not much else. From a biological point of view this is fine, but there are no school instructions on how to control kids hormones nor their desires to experience and indulge in sexual activity as that will be the responsibility of their parents.

In closing this discussion, parents need to inform their children of what appropriate sexual behavior is and what inappropriate behavior is about. For girls, mother's need to tell them to make sure they have and take precautions so as to avoid pregnancies, and tell your girls to be selective in the guys that she has sex with so as not to ruin their reputations. For boys becoming young men, fathers need to tell them to use protection when they have sex and to be gentle with the girls so as not to hurt them in anyway. In today's modern society and with the advent of computers, cell phones, and mini cameras, all parents need to make their kids aware of the fact that their sexual encounters could be displayed to the public on all these devices unbeknownst to them that could have devastating mental repercussions for your child if they are not aware of their situation and surroundings.

Any corrections that parents want to make concerning their kids should be done in an understanding manner and never from a controlling or forceful parental view point. The goal for parents is to get your kids to think about what they are about to do, and have the kids understand the possible consequences they could be subjected to by having sex. This would include: indulging in unprotected sex, pregnancies, or contracting various sexual diseases, not to mention the emotional aftermath that may occur. The older your kids become parents may want to suggest that their adolescent kids request a blood test report from the other person they may want to indulge in sexual activity with or suggest that they can both go together. Parents, this suggestion is just that, a suggestion that is designed to make your adolescent kids think before they indulge in any sexual activity. Asking for a blood test report is just a matter of precaution, but more than likely kids will not go through such a process as most sexual encounters are on the spur of the moment at their age. Even so, parents can explain to their adolescent kids that the reason for asking for a blood test is due to the fact that there are so many debilitating sexual diseases that are transmitted through sexual contact that could, in fact, cause death or shorten one's life span and their ability to ever have sex again, and if they do have sex again, thereby endangering another person's life, they could be prosecuted in a court of law for transmitting a sexual disease. This is not a very good or bright idea knowing that they could spend the rest of their lives behind bars because they knowingly infected another person.

Parents, when it comes to sex when your child or children enter their adolescence years, your best defense is going to be a great offense. By simply communicating with your child or children in a loving, caring, and in a logical way so they can understand and comprehend what a parent would like to relate to them concerning their thoughts about indulging in sexual activity will go a long ways in assisting them. We highly recommend that all parents invite their child or children to openly participate in this conversation so as not to have any misunderstandings and at the same time allowing your child or children to express their view points on this subject matter.

Furthermore, it is important for parents to allow their child or children to be the one who arrives at their own decisions and conclusions. Nevertheless, it will be crucial that parents do not attempt to discount, dismiss, disregard, or attempt to reject anything that your child or children may ask of you or relate to you concerning this subject matter. By the same token parents, give your child or children direct answers and if parents should not have or know the answer to any questions asked by their child or children, do not try to avoid or ignore the question, but be honest and tell your child or children that you will find the answer to their question and you will get back to them as soon as you can.

Remember parents, your child or children will be adequately well-developed in their minds and bodies at this stage of their lives and if you can't, or won't, or refuse to get an answer for them, I can guarantee you that your child or children will get the answer for themselves. The problem with this scenario is your child or children may get the wrong answers from someone else, which will then be the fault of the parents for not following up on a particular question. Commit this to memory parents, you only get one chance at being a parent or parents in your lifetime that will only last for a few years so make them the best years of your life for the betterment of your child or children.

CHAPTER 9

Kids Are A Mirrored Reflection of Their Parents

Anytime I would like to know how different parents are all I have to do is observe their children as they are a mirrored reflection of their parents. If children are mindful, polite, kind, and well-behaved, chances are their parents are the same. If children are loud, rude, and misbehaved, chances are their parents have acted the same way at one time or another. If children yell, scream, and run around uncontrolled, chances are that their parents have indulged in the same activities the same way at one time or another in front of their children. Allow me to give the reader an example: Recently, we went over to New Mexico to hunt for Finn's treasure and spent a week looking and after finding nothing, we finally came to the conclusion that even though Finn himself gave a lot of clues as to where his treasure may be located, we decided to leave it for some other lucky person as I was not interested in looking all over the Rocky Mountains for a little box even though it contained over a million dollars worth of coins, diamonds and jewelry.

While we were in Santa Fe we decided to look for a sporting goods store and found a Big 5 so we stopped and went in to look around. After a while I found some socks that were on sale for a buck a pair, normally marked 3 dollars a pair, so I bought 12 pairs. Stopping at the register to pay for the socks, some young guy about 25 or 26 started yelling at the cashier using some pretty foul language and as he was leaving the store, my son told my wife that this guy sounded just like his dad. This incident woke me up so as to start paying attention to what I was saying around my family and yet my so-called brain-damaged son was the one who brought this to my attention, but more on that in the next section. However, this just goes to show parents how your children can be a reflection of their parents. Fortunately for me, my son seems to ignore my outbursts and language when I become tired and frustrated, and he is lucky enough to be nothing like me because he is always kind, polite, and courteous to just about everyone and he avoids people he senses that are not amiable. Basically, parents form, mold, and determine the kinds of children they raise and how they raise them that will grow up and become a mirrored reflection of their parents up bringing.

PART 2

The Destructive World

Of

Cell Phones

When people go out to eat or to other places where people gather together, have you ever noticed how many people are on their cell phones, ignoring everyone around them? We see this all the time and it is destroying family values because there are no family values without socialization. These cell phones are literately destroying families because they separate family members from communicating and sharing one's day with each other and in essence isolating family members from each other, and then parents can't understand why they don't have any family cohesion. It's because everyone is living in their own world and they don't have time to be bothered or troubled by anything or anyone outside their own little world. Allow me to give the readers another example: About 11 years ago my family and I decided to move out of California because we wanted to retire and California was becoming too expensive for us so we moved to Texas. A few years later my daughter called us and stated that she was going to get married and invited the family to her wedding, but, unfortunately, we were still trying to get back on our feet in Texas and didn't have the money to attend her wedding. However, my daughter decided to bring her fiancé along with her to our place in Texas so that we could meet him. The guy was a nice guy, had a good education, and seemed responsible so we welcomed him into the family, but while they were visiting us, both my daughter and her soon to be husband spent the majority of their time on their phones. Now that my daughter was on her own I didn't say anything to her because they came to see a football game in Dallas and the next day they were gone, rather disappointing to say the least.

When we arrived in Texas and were settled in our home, we started to eat out everyday and that lasted for about 8 years when we finally sat down and figured out how much money this was costing us each month, and decided there are better things we could do with that money instead of wasting it on restaurants. However, during this time we would see entire families dinning together where everyone was on their cell phones, or texting, or checking messages and no one was talking to each other. No matter where we went people of all ages had cell phones glued to their ears and it looked like their phones were stuck to their heads and became their portable phone booth. Kids of all ages were being ignored as if they were the ones causing trouble, because mom would not put her phone down that was apparently attached to her head. The same goes for everyone else, to the point, that there is very little if any communication between family members today.

This phone addiction situation is out of control, so my wife and I decided to keep our outdated cell phone from 1996 and we still use it to this day. Nevertheless, when people come over to see us, we tell them to put their phones on vibration because we don't allow any modern cell phone usage in our home. As the readers can imagine, we are at a point now where no one ever comes over to see us and that is perfectly okay with us because we are not socialites and we detest cell phones in our presence when we decide to talk with people. If people can't keep their cell phones out of their ears when communicating with us, then we don't want or need them around us and this includes businesses. If people want a communication relationship with us, just leave your cell phone someplace where we won't hear them.

As far as kids are concerned, parents should not allow their kids to have cell phones until they are no longer under their parents direct control. Additionally, parents who decide to get cell phones for their kids should do so only if the kids may need the cell phone in an emergency situation, or have the cell phone restricted, using PhoneSheriff.com, which will restrict your child's texting and phone usage privileges that the parents can monitor. Granted that this cell phone with parental control will be short lived lasting for only a few years because as your child or children start growing, developing, and associating with their peer groups they will want a little more leeway with their cell phones the older they become. My solution to this situation was to tell my daughter that if she wanted her own cell phone that she was going to have to buy her own phone as I would not be responsible for her phone bills and would not co-sign for her to have a cell phone. In retrospect, this worked out just fine as my daughter did without a cell phone all the way through college, that we knew of anyways, and if she ever needed one, she would just borrow one from the people she knew.

PART 3

Learning to become Responsible

Like anything else children can and should be taught responsibilities at an early age, but with a lot of leeway in the child's early developmental phase of their lives, and increased as they grow and mature. Fortunately, this can be a fun learning process and experience for children as they love to mimic their parents and their activities. Boys will mimic their dads and girls want to mimic their moms and as time goes on both genders will grow closer together while children are in the early stages of their lives. However, like anything else caution is in order here so as not to discourage your children by constantly correcting them, putting them down, or yelling at them that will affect their learning abilities or scolding them because they may not have done something the parents wanted their children to do the right way according to the standards of the parents whatever they may be. Granted there are right and wrong ways to do certain things, but remember these are developing children of yours and you don't want them avoiding or shying away from responsibilities because you became too harsh on them.

In the early stages of their lives children will need constant encouragement and praises for any and all activities they may become involved in with their parents. When parents teach their children responsibility correctly, their children will want to take on more and more responsibility and the more confident they will become in their lives. As your children continue to grow and mature the easier it will become getting them to take on more and more responsibility, and some kids will develop a desire for wanting much greater responsibilities in order to demonstrate to their parents that they are ready and can handle any responsibility that comes their way. Again, parents have to be careful at this stage of their kids development because, technically, they are not yet ready for the responsibilities of the adult world even though they think they are at this stage in their lives. When my daughter was 14 years old, she asked if she could have braces and I told her in time because I did not have the money to pay for braces at that time. However, 2 years later she turned 16 and I told her that I would pay for her braces so we looked around and investigated several Orthodontists and interviewing each one until we finally found one who had a good reputation and seemed to answer all my questions with the right answers and we selected this particular Orthodontist for my daughter's braces.

Just before my daughter's high school graduation her teeth were completed and her braces came off and she was a very happy person. However, in order to prepare her for the responsibilities of the adult world, I went with her back to the Orthodontist for a followup checkup. When the checkup was finished, I informed the Orthodontist, with my daughter present, that I would no longer be financially responsible for any future followups for my daughter because she was now 18 years old and would now be financially responsible for any future orthodontic work she desired. Basically, it was now time for my daughter to take responsibilities for her own actions and decisions. Nonetheless, people would not believe the looks I received from the Orthodontist and his assistants when I told them that my daughter would be taking responsibility for herself and even handed them a letter indicating what I had said to them in writing. People react in different ways, but these people were in total disbelief and flabbergasted by what I had stated to them. Now, I would have thought they would have asked me why I had made this decision concerning my daughter, but the people had no ability to think outside the box, so to speak, and were not capable of understanding what I was teaching my daughter and since it was none of their business anyways, we just left the office while their mouths were hanging wide open in total disbelief. But, hey, they were too dumb to understand and rather feckless for not asking me any questions, not that I would tell them anything anyways because I didn't owe anyone any explanation in the first place. However, the end results of my decision turned out to be fantastic and astronomical for my daughter in the years to come.

If your kids decide to go to college, it may be okay, but parents today have to realize that their kids' brains are going to be filled with a lot of undesirable nonsense and information that will be the direct thoughts of their college instructors. Most kids are brainwashed in grade school and again at around 14 through 18 by their high school instructors. Nevertheless, should your kid decide to go to college, they will be under the tremendous influence of their instructors who will take over from the high-school-brainwashing teachers to become even more influential in your kids lives and will continue with even more brainwashing of your child, not to mention the interaction kids will be exposed to by the other students. Another example: I taught my daughter early on in her life to honor her parents, according to the Fifth Commandment of God's Ten Commandments because I was the one who would be taking care of her and her brother as long as they respected me while they would be living with me. Naturally, everything was fine up until my daughter entered San Diego State University. Whenever there would be a college break, my daughter would come home once in a while and wanted to stay with my wife and I and her brother before returning to college, and I told her it was perfectly fine.

My daughter said she would like to stay with us through the summer and we agreed. When she came home everything was fine until one day she decided to take a nap in her room and asked not to be bothered. Soon after, the phone rang and it was one of her friends so I opened her door very quietly and she appeared to be sleeping so I told her friend that she was sleeping and that I would tell her when she awoke and hung up. It was about 10 seconds later that my daughter came out of her room and told me that I was a liar. I immediately asked her what she had said to me and again she told me that I lied to whoever had called because she wasn't sleeping. First of all, I told her that I didn't have any idea that she was awake and, secondly, I told her that she had 15 minutes to gather her things and get out of my house because no one calls me a liar and gets away with it in my home, especially, being called a liar by my own daughter. When she asked me where she should go, I told her (in so many words) that I didn't care and to get out of my house and don't come back unless she wanted to apologize.

Come to find out about a little more than 6 months later, my daughter had observed some of her college friends talking back to their parents and bad mouthing them, so she thought she could do the same thing to me only to find out that she was sorely mistaken. Parents, allowing kids to mouth off to you or talk back to you is not a sign of respect or honor and should not be allowed by any parent or parents under any circumstances. Your kid or kids are to be taught and instructed as they are not in charge of raising their parents. Anyways, it was about 6 months or so later that my daughter came back from college again and apologized to me for what she had said and that she was staying with her mother. We told her that it was good to see her again and that was the end of our conversation for a long time to come, but eventually after her graduation from college we started talking again even though she remained with her mother where she had much more freedom to do what she wanted any time she wanted than she would have had living with me.

CHAPTER 10

Learning and Understanding Responsibility

Now that school was out of the way my daughter went looking for a job and like all college kids she felt that she should be compensated accordingly because she had a degree. Unfortunately, she had to learn the hard way that college degrees don't mean much other than telling people that she has the ability to read, learn, understand theory, follow directions, and, eventually, she got a job down at the docks gassing up boats and doing miscellaneous work around the little store that was located on the dock. It wasn't long before she called me asking what good did her degree do for her if she couldn't get a decent paying position. Even though I had no degrees at that time in my life and very little education, what I did have, was a tremendous amount of real life experience in all kinds of fields like, construction, heavy equipment operator, hand building swimming pools, selling business to business and house to house products, digging ditches, pipe laying, locksmithing, selling cars, becoming a Real Estate Loan Officer, operating printing presses, managing printing companies and owning a printing company, selling chemicals, only to become the vice president of a chemical company, and owning, operating, and writing a mortgage loan officer training manual, owning, operating and being the head instructor of the Professional Loan Officers Training Center where we trained over three quarters of all the brokers in Orange County, California at that time; owning a Real Estate company, a Mortgage Loan company, along with a Real Estate Loan Processing company, and the list goes on and on. Not to mention survival abilities that were learned in war torn Viet Nam in 1967 and a lot more. Basically, I was a walking encyclopedia specializing in functioning immediately in emergency situations, so I figured I'd offer my daughter some advice even though I told her that I would never interfere in her life ever again once she left our house and if she wanted any future advice, all she had to do was call and ask for it. Now that she was grown, I don't believe in interfering or becoming involved in other people's lives, including my own kids once they are out of my home and on their own. While I'm at it, the only other advice I gave my kid was that once she left my home she was to never come back unless she and her family wanted to visit.

Anyways, getting back to advising my daughter, I told her that she can forget about getting a position with any company unless she had some kind of contacts at any particular company. Secondly, I pointed out that even though she had some work experience while she was going to college that, basically, she didn't know anything or learn anything worthwhile when she was in college because they teach nothing but theory that has absolutely no use in the real working world because it is feckless information. All college teaches people is how to follow and tells people that they have the ability to follow and understand directions as long as someone's telling them what to do. Other than that, college is a waste of time, money, and energy, and yet kids still go to college for some unknown reason when the majority would be better off learning a trade at a trade school or have a lifetime of learning by someone they know or from their parents. Some of the most productive people we know are those who have learned on their own, and by their mistakes, have become successful at whatever it is they do and end up becoming leaders in their communities without having gone to college.

Now was the time to tell my daughter the facts of life concerning employment and I told her that there were only four ways she was going to get a position in any company and that was to be related to the owners, or maybe she had contact with one of the kids she went to college with that was in a company, or that had started or bought a company, or that she would get promoted to a position or she just gets lucky. Furthermore, I told her to get a job that she liked because she was not likely to get a position. Unfortunately, that is the way real life is and there was nothing she could do about it and I welcomed her to the real world. As time went on my daughter got working experience being a waitress, a marine manager, and an offer to move to some place in Chile to manage a boating rental company for the tourist trade in Chile that never amounted to anything. Next she got a job at a Beauty Salon as a front desk girl in a very wealthy area of Mission Viejo, California, and as time went on the owner of the salon happened to be the wife of the West Coast Saab Division Director located in Irvine, California.

Anyways, since there were only 3 people in the office they needed to replace the Administrative Specialist at the West Coast Saab Division. When this guy mentioned this to his wife, she immediately mentioned my daughter as she was very impressed with her and her capabilities and the husband told his wife to have her come in for an interview. The Director conducted a round table interview with all three of the applicants. Now mind you my daughter is only 23 years old having limited experience and wanted to know what she should do and wear to such an interview. I told my daughter to wear clothing that was appropriate for the business world. My daughter went to the interview and was asked for a second interview as the Director was interviewing all over Irvine, California, for this position. Before the second interview my daughter wanted to know what she should say and I told her to just listen to what he has to say and simply answer his questions. Next I told her to ask the Director of Saab if corporate offered stock incentives, employee matching 401K programs, or other retirement programs, and to ask what kind of health plans Saab had to offer their employees. Now, even though my daughter may have known a little bit about these subjects, these were questions that any employee would know something about, let alone a young girl, but these questions were designed to get this guy's attention and put my daughter into the forefront for the position. Two days later my daughter received a call stating that she had been picked for another interview that was to be a phone interview with Human Resources located at Saabs Headquarters in Georgia.

After answering the questions she asked them what the salary range was and they responded with $35,000.00 annual salary. A week later my daughter was called back and told that she would be starting at $45,000.00 and my daughter asked why? The HR person at Saab stated that she was being hired as a temporary without benefits and that the extra monies were so that my daughter could buy her own benefits. Needless to say, my daughter was excited that she got the position and I told my daughter to come with me the next day and we went to Ann Taylors and got her a personal assistant who I told to dress my daughter as an executive and that I would be deciding whether her clothing was appropriate or not for the business world. About three and a half hours later my young daughter not only looked like an administrative specialist, but she acted like one. I was happy for her even though it cost me a small fortune for girls' clothes that I never had to pay for guys' clothes, but she looked and felt great and that is all that counted and mattered to me. However, I did tell her that this was a one time shopping spree and that she would have to pay for her own clothes from now on.

While my daughter was working at Saab in Irvine, California, General Motors bought out Saab and everyone was asked to move to Thousand Oaks, California, if the people wanted to keep their jobs. When she transferred to Thousand Oaks with GM she became a full time employee and, therefore, had to be given full company benefits. The nice part about all this is that my daughter reaped the benefits including keeping her salary and not having to buy her own benefits anymore. When my daughter called and told me the good news, not only was I happy for her, but I now knew that she was on her way in the world and would no longer need me unless she needed additional advice in the future. I had done my job well raising my daughter and my daughter had learned well and now understood what responsibility is all about. Now it is her turn to instruct and train her own daughter the way I trained her, but with much more and even better understanding and parenting abilities that I had to learn the hard way through trial and error.

How your children are raised is the direct responsibility of the parents and should never be left up to the school teachers or anyone else for that matter because other people's ideas can be completely different from the parents. For years I fought the school systems concerning my kids as I did not care for the way some of their instructors were directing my children and I made it a point to tell them my view point. Most of the time the people in charge at the schools corrected the instructors who would be out of line, and sometimes I had to threaten the people in charge that if they didn't correct a problem instructor, that I would call the local police to have the instructor corrected. Naturally, when I got to this point, I had their complete attention and cooperation, and everything was immediately taken care of including having teachers fired for inappropriate behavior. Because of my background with teachers, I had very little patience when it came to incompetent teachers that wanted to force our children to think the way they thought, thereby undermining and eroding the parents instructional abilities. In other words, these teachers want your kids to ignore what they are being taught by their parents and to follow their way of thinking and how they perceive things.

Another thing a parent or parents need to be aware of, especially, if they have above average intelligent kids in the third or fourth grades at their schools that they may be put into a class along with the slower and less intelligent kids. This situation happened to my daughter in the fourth grade when she had come home from school and I asked her how she did on her first day in her fourth grade class. When she started to tell me about her day she indicated that it was okay, but that her and only two other girls were the only caucasian kids in her class and that the rest of the class was all hispanic. Talk about being manipulated, the school put these three intelligent girls in a class with some poorly educated hispanic kids in the anticipation that these girl's would have the ability to bring these other kids up to their standards. To say I was infuriated would be to put it mildly to think that this school was willing to sacrifice my daughter's intelligence and her 4-point grade average in order to help these less educated children by becoming a quasi teacher was ludicrous to say the least. It is a proven fact that taking above average intelligent kids and placing them with less intelligent kids will cause smart kids to regress down to the intelligence level of these poorly educated ones. The first thing I did the following day was to take my daughter to her school and demanded to see the principal. After conversing with the principal I gave him one day to transfer my daughter out of this class and placed into a better class with kids of her intelligence or else I would pull my daughter out of school and sue the school for malfeasance and malice for attempting to use my daughter as a quasi teacher; my daughter was transferred back that same day with her regular class students.

As a parent you may go along with this manipulation by the school system, but my kids were not going to be brainwashed into believing that they should change their thought processes to the way their teachers wanted them to think. In my opinion, this is and has been the major contribution to the problems our kids are facing today because these teachers have brainwashed these kids into believing they should THINK the way they think. Unfortunately, your kids and parents have not been made aware of this propaganda process being used by our school systems. Parents must realize that someone is always going to try, including other children, to convince your children that their way is a better way to think and do things and that your children should follow their lead. If parents do their job correctly, they will have raised their children to develop their own thought processes and they will be able to analyze each and every situation that they might or may encounter at home and in the school system. The problem area starts from kindergarten through to the sixth grade where your child's brain can be molded very easily by teachers, and the students who go along with the teachers' brainwashing techniques simply don't understand what is happening to them. This is where parenting abilities will be most important, and all you have to do is to communicate with your children when they come home from school each and every day by asking them what they learned at school that day. By asking your children what they liked and didn't like about their teacher and school each day, parents will be able to correct and assist their children in understanding what their teacher may have been trying to get across to your children without offending anyone at their school. Using a question and answer system with your children, parents are then able or should be able to adjust their children's understanding of what they were told in school that can be turned around by parents countering their children's teacher's propaganda in the way that parents want their children to understand what is taking place in their school system. In other words, parents will have direct control over what their children will be learning even if it doesn't agree with what their children are being taught and exposed to by the school systems. We know that this reverse psychology will take a lot of time, but parents will be able to direct their children's social outlook, understanding, and responsibilities the way the parents want their children to develop and not the way the school system wants for your children to develop or the way teachers think your children should learn, understand, and deal with responsibilities. It is also of vital importance that parents tell their children not to say anything to their teachers about their home discussions because this may get them into trouble at school by their teachers. Just teach your kids to remember what they talked about at home and to forget what they talked about when they get to school. It is the parents' choice, they can raise their children and control how they will grow up to view their outlook of society, with understanding, and how parents would like their children to handle responsibilities, or parents can do nothing and allow the school system to raise your children by propagandizing them with their distorted ideas.

Unfortunately, today the majority of teachers don't just teach their subject to their students anymore without putting in their own two cents of what they may think and believe in thereby indoctrinating our kids to their ways of thinking regardless of how distorted their thought processes may be. If teachers would do what they are paid to do and just teach the subject matter they were hired to teach and keep their mouths shut about everything else going on in the world that they know nothing about, including their own personal opinions, then our school systems and our society would be a much better place to get along in. This, especially, includes foreign teachers who have come from different countries and backgrounds who attempt to impart their ideas and thoughts on our children's thinking that it is the right thing to do, which they are sorely mistaken. These teachers are just like any one of the other teachers and should be instructed to keep their thoughts, ideas, and opinions to themselves and just do what they were hired to do, and that is to teach the subject they know and are proficient at to our children. Consequently, and as a result of my dealing with teachers from grade school, junior high, and high school I only ran across one competent teacher in the forth grade who really cared about her students assisting them to achieve the best they could based on their abilities. Unfortunately, the rest of the teachers were more interested in being something they were not, but acted as if they were way above and beyond the students they were supposed to be teaching. The majority of these teachers expected to be respected and yet they were feckless, incompetent, and pompous having no business teaching in my opinion.

PART 2

Raising Children

To Be

Efficient and Competent

When I was raising my children, I would always encourage them to complete whatever project they were involved in and see to it that they did whatever it was as efficiently as they were capable of doing it with encouragement. Never did I point out negatives to them and I always taught them to be positive people regardless of what other people may think or say about of them. I also taught them to ignore people and their comments, regardless of what they may have been, and never worry about what other people may think of them. This is a process I learned a long time ago that has served me and my kids well and as long as we didn't care whatever other people thought we managed to accomplish whatever it was we were doing without listening to other people's input. By having my children ignore other people's criticism and feckless innuendoes, they were able to concentrate on whatever it was they were doing and over time both of them became very efficient and competent at whatever task they undertook for whatever reason. This also included not listening to anyone who might attempt to persuade them to try something like pills, cocaine, other drugs or any other substances just so they could be part of a group which is pure nonsense. Parents, warning kids about these situations will be one of the smartest decisions any parent can do for their children.

The goal behind my parenting process was to eventually raise my children to become smarter and brighter people than I was, so that they could take on anything and be proud of what they had become and proficient at their achievements. This I hope would be the goal of any parents in order to give their children a fighting chance at advancing in anything your own children decide to undertake in their lives for the benefit of themselves, their families, and others. However, in order to accomplish this parenting feat it will require a lot of rethinking, reevaluating, and realignment of one's thought process of the way they were brought up as children in order to embrace a better and different way to raise their own children without malice or malediction.

Over the years we have seen people grow up only to become statistics of incarceration, substance abuse, alcoholics, child abuse, and child murderers that can all be traced back to the way they were raised by their parents. We have seen what were smart bright kids in school winning all kinds of accolades only to become grown people that could not make it in the real world. The majority of them became homeless people, street bums, and people who just gave up on the system all because of the way they were raised. Parents, raising children to become losers is a relatively easy task for any parents to achieve without much effort. Regrettably, the only one that suffers is the grownup child that remains a grownup child who doesn't learn and is incapable of adjusting to the demands of the everyday adult life. As an example: Recently we heard of a very intelligent person having several degrees including three Ph.D's that was unable to succeed in any endeavor he ever attempted in the working world and ended up living as a homeless person. As sad as this may seem to have such a very brilliant person like this having to live on the streets of America, we sincerely hope this will not happen to your child, and as parents, you can adjust to a better way of raising well-rounded children that look forward to different challenges now and in their future to come.

Parents, we live in a very fast moving and developing world that will require your every effort to raise your child or children in such a way as to make them prepared to compete in this world and overcome any and all obstacles that may come their way. In order to accomplish this undertaking will require proper instructions, knowledge, skills, education, proficiencies, and a lot more, including the acumen required to survive in this world of ours. All parents should have as their goals to raise smarter and brighter kids than they are because their adventure will just be starting while your adventures as a parent or parents will be coming to an end, hopefully, not too soon. The future of your child or children will be in your parenting abilities and will depend on how well you are able to convey these instructional concepts to them that they will hopefully follow in their endeavors in whatever adventures that they undertake and strive for in their lives. The child or children of a parent or parents who achieve these goals will now have young adults that can pass this education and experience on to their child and children if and when they ever decide to start or have their own families.

CHAPTER 11

Welcome To The Wonderful World of Lying

Parents can call lying by all sorts of names like untruth, fibbing, white lies, fabricating, deceit, mendacity, and many more names, but it all comes down to not telling the truth or trying to hide the truth and everyone does it whether they want to admit it or not. Kinda of like what Jesus stated in John 8:7 when people were going to stone a woman, which was "Let any one of you who is without sin be the first to throw a stone at her," and everyone dropped their stones and walked away because everyone sins. How about the Garden of Eden where the very first lie was spoken to God by Eve who then implicated Adam in her lie by giving the forbidden fruit to Adam who also took a bite. Since Eve, women have become the most creative liars in the world, but they like to say that it was only a simple misrepresentation or terms to that effect, but regardless of what terms people use, it is still a lie. Even God knew lying was going to be a problem for all mankind so he made and issued the 9th Commandment that states: "You shall not give false testimony against your neighbor." However, looking up neighbor in the Bible we found it to mean everyone and not just anyone's neighbor as the majority of people believe the 9th commandment to indicate by viewing these words from a literal point of view. In other words everyone is your neighbor.

Children usually learn to start lying, depending on the intelligence of the child, as early as 3 and 5 years old and the process of lying usually exists all throughout a person's lifetime. However, the question is why, simple, self-preservation. Yes, but why? According to the definition: "Lying is the protection of one's self from harm and is regarded as a basic instinct in human beings." Yes, but why do children begin lying? Good question, so let's explore some reasons children lie. Remember Chapter 7, where we talked about children being a mirrored reflection of their parents? This is where children learn to lie, from their parents. Parents, you need to understand that all children at a very early stage of their lives are constantly observing their parents' activities. If the parents lied about something that their children observed and they know it was not true or correct even though they may be too young to totally understand, this event will be filed into their little developing brains and guaranteed to emerge at a later time. Simply through the observation of the parents, children are learning to lie and some will become rather good at lying over time, but remember it is from you, the parents, where children learn to lie.

So what are parents to do when their children first begin to lie or like I asked my kids, "Are you telling me a story?" How parents react when they first catch their children in a lie will make all the difference in yours and their lives, not to mention how your children will respond as they grow and develop their thought processes. When I first caught my son and daughter telling me a lie, I just asked them if they were telling me a story? Depending on whether they would tell me the truth or try and lie again, I simply told them that I had been watching and heard them at that time. When my children were 3 and 5 years of age, I would just tell them that I would appreciate it much better if they would tell me the truth, and if and when they did tell me the truth, I would thank them for it and let them go about their business. On the other hand, if they tried to lie to me again, I would just make them sit in the chair until they picked their punishment, and most of the time they would just be sent to their rooms for a while to think about what happened to them for not telling me the truth when I gave them a second chance.

Should any parent physically correct their child or children at such early ages for lying, beware that your children will retaliate against you and grow up to be constant liars in order to avoid any physical punishment. Unfortunately, some parents think physical punishment will correct the lying process, but in reality what parents are doing is making the problem worse. As we mentioned early on in this book if parents don't have the intelligence to outthink and outsmart little children, then they have no business having children. In my situation I would have to estimate that 99% of the time or better that my kids told me the truth all the time because they knew that I would not put my hands on them and that they were responsible for their actions. Furthermore, my kids were never afraid or had any fear of me that would cause them to want to lie to me or my wife even though I was a very demanding father. Children or kids who develop a fear of talking to their parents or are afraid of any repercussions that may come their way, will always lie to their parents knowing that they can avoid a beating. The reason I know this is because I had to become an expert liar in order to avoid continued beatings when I was growing up in our household.

The best way that I have found to deal with my kids lying was to constantly communicate with them instructing them to think and use their own reasoning as to why they did the things that they did. Parents that allow their kids to think through any problems that they encounter will be greatly rewarded in the long run simply because their kids are not afraid, fearful, terrified, scared, or frightened, of their parents. When kids don't have any anxieties concerning their parents, they technically will not have any need to tell lies to their parents. Parents utilizing this approach when their kids first start lying will end up finding it far more gratifying as their kids continue to grow up because their kids will be more truthful with their parents. Please don't get me wrong as your kids will eventually lie to people for one reason or another just like everyone else does in this world of ours.

How kids will deal with lying will depend on how their parents reacted when they were first caught lying for whatever reason. When my kids caught me lying to someone I would tell them the reason I lied or that it was better for the person I lied to so as not to hurt their feelings. I also taught my kids that there would be times when it is better to lie to someone so as not to scare them or create any animosity in a particular situation, but if I could avoid lying, I usually tell the truth even though it might upset or bother the person I was talking to. Parents must also realize that lying to their kids may eventually come back to bite them once the kids learn the truth concerning whatever the situation was that parents had to lie to their kids about at the time. If it is at all possible, parents, try to avoid lying to or in front of your children and teach them a better way to deal with a situation where they may decide to lie in order to get out of a jam, but if the situation calls for lying, then so be it.

Nevertheless, whatever parents do, don't and we mean don't attempt to correct your kids by physically punishing them and do your best to outthink and out-smart your kids. Remember, your kids may hopefully be around for all of you to enjoy for a lifetime because, believe me, your children will grow up in a hurry and before you realize it they are moving out of what used to be their home living with you as their parents. One of the greatest accomplishments a parent or parents can ask for is for their children to always want to come back home to visit and share their lives with their parent or parents.

CHAPTER 12

How To Handle The Problem Child

In this section parents will learn why and how children become problem children and it is mostly caused by the parents, but there are outside influences that can cause kids to become problem children. Unfortunately, we get back to that word "NO" again as this word is also an exclusionary and not an inclusive or in any way a positive word. However, parents need to realize that children who are constantly told "No" will themselves start to become negative children making it difficult for them to develop their self-confidence. This in turn may lead to a child lashing out to become a problem child by biting, yelling, screaming, hitting, kicking, or crying, and displaying other forms of abrasive, abusive, or aggressive, behavior towards their parents, siblings, and other children. This is a sign of immaturity and bad behavior that has become an epidemic in our society today because parents are afraid of what other people will think of them should they correct their children when they are in public. When either one of my children made attempts at misbehaving, I simply snapped my fingers, put them in the vehicle, and removed them from the public as fast as I could. When we got home it was now chair time and question and answer time. Once we discovered what the problem or cause was and how it was created all that was left was for my kid, whichever one it was, to let them decide what their punishment should be and that was the end of that and no more problem.

Parents must understand that using the word "No" will delay a child's overall development, and when the time eventually comes for their kids to become independent, they will be too immature to grasp that idea and will most likely fail at just about everything they try to do on their own. As long as someone is there to assist, guide, and instruct these kids they will be all right, but what happens when no one is around to offer these kids assistance? They will become problems for themselves and others that are around them. So, as parents what do we do? If parents haven't trained their children at the earliest stages before birth or as soon after birth as possible giving your children praises, encouragement, acceptance, recognition, and approvals, and lots of love and kindness, then parents may have to eventually seek out professional help. One of the worst sayings we have heard from parents is that, "Our children are just going through a growing stage," talk about ignorant parents, they are ignoring the signs that there may in fact be something wrong with their child or children.

Our suggestion is for parents to pay attention to their children and communicate with them to determine, if in fact, there is a problem that has become repetitive that your child may or may not be aware of or that has not been brought to their attention. More than likely these problems were never made aware of to your child and when they are confronted with their problem, it usually goes away. However, if after parents notice their child did not correct the problem after 2 or 3 months, depending on the severity of the problem, then professional assistance may be required. Parents, getting professional assistance for your child should not be a long drawn-out process regardless of what the professional may think, but a good qualified professional may be able to solve the problem in one or two sessions as long as they know what they are talking about. Remember, these people make their living counseling people and if they can con or rather convince you that your child will require several sessions, just thank them for their time and find another counselor. On the other hand, if your child is of school age, the school should have a list of counselors that your child can visit at a reduced rate or for free.

PART 2

Sibling Rivalry

The more children parents have the more likely they are going to deal with sibling rivalry depending on how each of your kids are raised, and hopefully, they will all receive the same loving kindness, attention, encouragement, and recognition they all deserve. In this situation parents should seldom experience any sibling rivalry. On the other hand, for the parents who do not or have not attempted an alternative method of training their children then they will experience a lot of sibling rivalry that can turn very violent at times. The first time I encountered this situation was when I was about 5 or 6 years old when I had an argument with my older brother years ago in the fifties. Anyways, whatever this disagreement may have been about has long been forgotten, but the brain doesn't forget the consequences of a violent situation. Nevertheless, somehow our dad got involved and took us out on the patio and instructed us to fight each other with our bare fists to clear whatever problems we were having. To say the least, my older brother, who was 2 years older than me and a head taller than me, beat the dickens out of me that set me on a path of revenge and stored up anger in me along with a desire for payback and that aggressive behavior has never gone away. For our old man to have allowed this to take place early on in my development set me on a path for revenge that I still have not been able to ignore or control to this very day. This single event would turn my life into a nightmare for any parent to have to deal with and I didn't even realize it at the time.

Basically, this incident turned me into a very deceptive, cunning, belligerent, pugnacious and confrontational person having a very distorted thought process that would last into my twenties and was buried deep within my brain. Furthermore, I made up my mind that I would never let anyone try to destroy my spirit ever again no matter what I did or had to endure as I was growing up. Because of this one single incident, somehow or someway, I started developing a very analytical and logical thought process that remains with me to this day. What my old man made us do to each other should tell parents why there is a better way to raise your children. Because of an on-going situation like this one I gave both my parents an "F" in parenting, and after returning from Viet Nam I never did maintain any relationship with either of my parents again. When I had my kids I only took them over to see their grandparents once or twice and never again because I never wanted them exposed to any of his sick demeanors. Although I did not allow the old man to go to his grave without letting him know what I really thought of him for what he did to me, thereby getting back at him for all the years of brutal mistreatment I received from him, and it was like a huge weight lifted off my conscious and subconscious brain and I could start thinking straight again.

The reason I mentioned this is because I want parents to know and understand how they can set in motion a disturbing situation by not being considerate towards their children. Another thing that played on my mind was when my parents would tell me they did the best they could raising me. From my view point, this was a pure outright lie because there was available help out there that could have resolved my problems, but our parents were not willing to pay for any professional outside assistance. Thinking about this situation years later, I came to the conclusion that the reason my parents didn't seek assistance for me was because they did not want anyone else finding out how my brothers and I were being treated by our parents while growing up. Therefore, if people are planning on having children, they should first decide if a child will openly be welcomed into their family with love, kindness, and given all the consideration they require. Parents should also consider discussing their partner's parental thoughts, ideas, and viewpoints on how they would consider raising children along with discussing how they were raised by each of their families. This in turn will assist both people in deciding how they plan on raising their children together instead of having kids just because it may have been an accident, but instead based on their sound judgements and desires. Likewise, even if it was an accident and your baby is brought into this world, it does not give a parent the right to physically harm, abuse, mistreat, or condemn any child in any way under any circumstances whatsoever.

PART 3

Other Factors That Can Cause Problem Children

In the beginning of this Chapter we mentioned that there may be some outside influences that can cause kids to become problem children for parents. One of the biggest problems of our modern society is the medical establishment that is harming more and more kids today with their vaccines. Allow me to give parents some statistics stated by the American Medical Association (AMA) that indicates that 50% of all children today develop a chronic disease caused by vaccines. Vaccinations are responsible for killing over 28,000 babies before their first birthday and the number is increasing. The current rate of Autism caused by vaccines today is currently 1 in every 45 kids and 21% of all kids are developmentally disabled each year by vaccines. As if these statistics were not bad enough as they are, the CDC and pharmaceutical companies are constantly pushing flu shots for kids that increases their chances of developing diabetes, and taking 5 consecutive annual flu shots increases a person's chances of developing Dementia and Alzheimers by 75%; hence, the reason for all the Alzheimers and Dementia care facilities suddenly popping up all over the country. Parents may now be asking, why hasn't anyone tried to stop this madness, and yet the answer is simple, it is called money and the greed out ways the problems that vaccines cause because it is big, big business.

It is one thing for children to develop problems that technically can be resolved by confronting them with their problem in an understanding way, or by seeking assistance for them in order to resolve a child's problem. However, it will become a major problem for parents should their children develop any problems that may be caused by vaccinations. In the 50's all kids received only 5 vaccinations, in the 60's the number increased to 8, and in the year 2010 vaccinations increased to a minimum of 13 or almost two and a half times more than from the 1950s. Parents should also be made aware of the fact that there are now only 6 vaccines required by law for kids entering child care, depending on their age at the time of their enrollment. Only 5 vaccinations are required for kids entering Kindergarten and only 2 more for those entering the 7th grade. However, every state has different requirements for children vaccination guidelines so be sure to check with your state's Public Health Department for your child's required immunizations. Other than these 13 immunizations being required by law, parents should always question any doctors recommending any additional immunizations for your kids contrary to the state's immunization requirements, and don't hesitate to say, "No" to the doctors regardless of what kind of explanation they try to persuade parents to go along with concerning your children because this is money in their pockets. Parents should also be aware of the fact that approximately 80% of all doctors are on pharmaceutical companies' payrolls and the number is increasing because it is lucrative for them to push drugs and vaccines.

In fact, it is advisable for all people to tell their doctors that their doctor is allowed to suggest, advise, and offer alternatives to you, regardless of your medical situation or condition, and tell them that you will be the one who will approve or disapprove their advice or recommendations since it is your body or your children's bodies. My wife and I have been using this doctor notification process for years and it has worked exceptionally well for us as it causes doctors to think before they make a recommendation concerning our health. We are both in our 70's and neither one of us is on or takes any kind of drugs even though people age 60 and older are on 12 to 16 or more drugs per day according the AMA. Another little known fact put out by the AMA stated that, "The leading cause of death in the US is Medical Care." I don't know about the readers, but this information doesn't give me a warm fuzzy thought process and that is why I always carry a Medical Power of Attorney with me wherever I go, mainly for protection against the medical establishment. Parents, vaccinations can cause a myriad of mental and physical damage in children and the sad part about all of this is that parents usually don't know where or how the problem started or developed. Again, our recommendation for parents is to maintain a dated record of any vaccinations that their children may be given in the event that your child has a reaction that causes a problem down the road giving parents the ability to trace whatever the problem was caused by. Unfortunately, pharmaceutical and vaccine companies are no longer liable or allowed to be sued here in the US and held accountable for their drugs and vaccines, but hopefully this will all change in the future. In the meantime it is the parents who will have to suffer and take care of their children affected by immunizations. In essence, the human body was not made to endure a multitude of foreign chemicals being introduced into the body, and having a foreign chemical introduced into the human body that alters its physiology violates biological law.

Parents, the bottom line to this situation is to go along with your state's mandated immunization requirements and then protect your children from any further immunization that may be recommended by any doctor or others practicing in the medical field. Likewise, unless it is a mandated immunization by your state there is no need to listen to anything your schools may try to convince you of indicating that your children may also require additional immunizations. In other words, if the immunization is not mandated by state law, parents have the legal right of refusal on behalf of their children. Should the school administration indicate that your children will not be allowed to attend school unless parents agree to immunize their children, then parents should bring a law suit against the school system as this is coercion under duress and it is illegal. Children who develop mental and physical problems caused by immunizations can face a lifetime of problems that can break parents physically, mentally, and financially even with all the help that is available today. So, it is our opinion that parents protect their children from the medical and pharmaceutical industries at all costs.

Parents, it is also important to note that kids today can be harassed and bullied by their classmates to the point of driving them to commit suicide, or as we have all seen, driving kids to the point of killing their classmates as a means of retaliation because they were not capable of thinking their way out of these kinds of situations. Parents who have their children's best interest and wellbeing foremost in their minds should or will know or suspect when something may be affecting your children's attitudes and behavior. At this point, parents can intervene right away to assist their children with whatever problems they may be encountering whether at school or elsewhere. However, parents, never demand your children to give you the information that is bothering them, but rather gently prod, guide, and encourage them to allow you, as parents, to assist them with their problems. Another outside influence that can affect your children and cause them to become problem children is other children or older kids that are vying for your kids attention for one reason or another. This, unfortunately, is the situation I found myself in when I started hanging out with the wrong kids. Even though these were bad kids having no morals or ethics they nevertheless paid attention to me so I would join their gang which I, eventually, did. Was this a smart move? At the time, it was a great move on my behalf because these kids made me feel welcomed unlike my parents or other people. These gang members were never abusive, rude, abrasive, disrespectful, or vituperative towards me and they made me feel welcomed as if I was someone that meant something to them and the other members that never happened to me while living with my parents.

Despite all of that, I started heading down the wrong path with these guys because I had no idea of what was really happening. Even though I never did get caught doing anything serious, these guys taught me all sorts of criminal activities that they took for granted and, eventually, I did too. At the time, one of the nice things about being a member of a gang was that no one bothered me and if they did, they had the rest of the gang to deal with any problems that may have confronted any one of us. Unlike our parents, once we were outside and out of our parents surroundings, we could and would do whatever it was that we wanted to with no worry of any kind of repercussions.

Parents must realize that paying attention to their children and treating them with love, kindness, and consideration will stop kids from seeking other outside outlets to make themselves believe they are real people having a real purpose in life other than being beaten, yelled at, or subjected to abusiveness. This is just another example of how your children can turn into problem children if parents don't treat their children correctly. Furthermore, there already exist a myriad of outside sources vying for your kids attention and if the parents don't pay attention to their children, I can guarantee you that your child or children will become a problem. The only question will be, are you ready for the challenge to become a great parent or will you, like the multitude of other parents, fall to the wayside and let your children seek and search for outside influences that could very easily turn them into a problem child? Only you, the parent or parents, can and will be able to answer that question depending on how devoted you are to raising your child or children or you can let the legal system do it for you, your choice.

CHAPTER 13

A Parent's Worst Nightmare

It is not my intention to scare or frighten soon to be parents or current parents, but by revealing a little bit about what can happen to parents if they create a problem child by raising them in a non-loving, non-kind, non-considerate, and non-affectionate home environment that may, hopefully, change parents' minds about abusing their children even when they think it is the right way to raise their children. These are true events that happened to me, the author of this book, as I was raised along with my 3 brothers by our parents in our home environment.

It all started in Pasadena and Altadena, California, where both my older brother and myself were born two years apart in the same hospital only 8 beds apart from where my older brother was born in Pasadena and I was born in Altadena because the hospital was on the Pasadena dividing city line according to our birth certificates. Naturally, I had no idea of these events, and it wasn't until a few years had gone by that I had learned from my older brother that I had been dropped by our old man from about waist high when I was a little over a year old according to my older brother who had witnessed this event of which I had no knowledge of at the time that this event even took place. Whether or not this event had any affect on my brain or may have contributed to the way I turned out as a kid only God could answer that question. However, as time went on I really had no recollection of my early childhood until I entered Kindergarten in Arizona where my parents had moved taking my older brother and myself with them.

My first foray leading me into a life of petty crimes was started by a teacher I had in kindergarten where she made an incursion into my life in the school cafeteria when she attempted to force me to eat the spinach on my lunch tray, even after I told her that I didn't like spinach. This kindergarten teacher didn't care and forced me to eat the spinach until I threw up the rest of my lunch along with the spinach all over the lunch table listening to the other kids saying ooh. Little did this brainless teacher realize that she had declared war on herself and all I could think about while I was in the nurse's office was how to get even with this teacher who assaulted me for no reason. Over the years I have learned that teachers can make or break children just as fast as parents can. Unfortunately, and because of this school incident I became my own epidemic of bad misbehavior and aggressiveness towards any and all teachers and anyone else who thought they had control over me and thought they could tell me what I could and could not do. Fortunately for me, none of these people could read my mind because if they could, I would have been committed a long time ago in my early childhood.

Nevertheless, it would only be a matter of time before I got even with this teacher. I had very little friends and really developed a dislike for most of the rest of the kids that were in my age group due to the way they acted and how they submitted to authority. However, I still managed to develop a couple of close relationships with other male kids, as I had no use for girls in kindergarten and besides, girls just seemed to want to do girly things. Okay, getting back to this evil teacher, as I was observing her behavior I noticed her spending a lot of time in her purse so I decided to find out what was so enticing in her purse. I got one of my friends to act as a decoy right outside the classroom while I went through this teacher's purse. Granted little kids don't know much about girly things, but we do know about money and so I helped myself to some of hers and only left her the large bills like 10's and 20's because at my age I didn't have any idea of what these bills were good for. My plan went off without a hitch and as an added measure I took her keys and threw them in a school trash can, but, unfortunately, the school janitor found them and they were returned to her.

That incident was the beginning of what was to come and I never did get caught, like my daughter did, so to me there was no limit to what I could get away with. The reader already knows about the fight that took place with my older brother and the severe beating I was given as a little kid by our old man, so moving on, second and third grades were okay, but that year we moved to a little town called Clawson located in Michigan in 1959. I turned 10 in 1959 and fell into the wrong crowd of kids that led me to developing some very bad traits and I even made my first zip gun when I was about 12 or 13 and fired 38's out of it. As the years rolled by our little group decided to form our own gang that was comprised of about 7 or 8 of us kids at that time. Naturally, this also led to developing some more very bad habits like smoking since we all started emulating the dress code of Fonzie in Happy Days played by Henry Winkler but, hey, we were still just kids becoming mean kids.

It was interesting to note that while we were still in Arizona my mother started to take up smoking and one day going down the hallway in our home, I noticed this smoke coming out of my mother's mouth. This event really fascinated me so I decided to go take a closer look when I saw the old man talking to her on the end of their bed. So, not thinking much about this event I walked up and asked my mother if I could have a taste? The reaction I got from the old man was immediate outrage directed at me as I was told that if the old man ever caught me smoking, that he would beat me within an inch of my life. Now, as a parent one would think that this would be enough of a threat to scare a kid, right? No way, for me this became a challenge because I figured that if it was okay for my mother to smoke, then it was okay for me to smoke. Again, someone was trying to control me instead of reasoning with me and in my mind I was going to learn how to smoke just like my mother sooner or later and no one was going to stop me.

Incidentally, this exact situation occurred with my daughter and because I became a smoker only with a completely different results. One day my daughter caught me smoking when she was about 5 or 6 and she asked me if she could have a taste and I told her sure, but first I had to show her how to smoke. I then showed her how to suck the smoke out of the cigarette and how to inhale deeply and she said she understood so I gave her the cigarette and away she went. The next thing I knew she started choking and coughing and with her eyes running she couldn't get away from the cigarette fast enough. By doing this I solved two future potential problems, one being that my daughter would never take up smoking or try to smoke cigarettes again and, secondly, she learned not to take people at face value no matter what they say. The way I conducted this situation with my daughter would have worked just as well with me, as well as, any other kid had my parents had the ability to think before reacting with irrational threats at the time. To this day my daughter does not smoke nor does she have any desire to smoke. This goes to show parents that there are better ways of treating and raising children that doesn't require physical punishment as parents should never put their hands on any of their children, but rather outthink, outsmart, educate, and train them by letting them come to their own conclusions and to stand by their decisions, be these right or wrong. However, if your children are right, be sure to praise and encourage them and if they are wrong, be sure to explain why you as parents believe they are wrong and why. This in turn will cause kids to be understanding and become thinkers instead of rebellious children.

Another situation that parents should know about is when kids start viewing their own bodies and discovering themselves. I remember being in the bathtub taking a bath when I started discovering myself or as some parents back then called it playing with oneself when all of a sudden I heard the old man's voice asking me what the so and so I was doing? Naturally, I responded with "Nothing" and then was told that if I ever did that again that I would get beaten within an inch of my life. Come to think about it, I think this was the old man's favorite phrase. In any event, not only did this make me more curious about my body, but it created a sexual desire in me for some unknown reason to want to know more about the opposite sex and what my penis was really designed for. As time went on and I got older and being a rather good looking kid, I had lots of girls who wanted to be my girlfriends. I, on the other hand, wanted to know more about girls bodies so I would make them a deal and told them I would allow them to be my girlfriend only if I could feel them up. At that time it was amazing to learn just how many girls agreed to my terms as fast as they did, and I had a secret place in the woods where I would conduct my exploration of the female body.

Over time I became better and better at pleasing girls and making them feel good, but I never did have sex until I was 17 years old and in the military for some unknown reason other than having been threatened by my old man early on in my life. Likewise, I want to point out to parents the way I handled this situation with my two kids when I first caught them exploring themselves at very young ages. First was my son when I happened to walk in on him while he was taking a bath and noticed him exploring his body sex organ. When he saw me, I told him, in a very calm voice, that if it felt good to him, then by all means do it if it makes you feel good and that was that. It has been over some 41 years later and I never did see my son exploring himself again, which means he doesn't still do it, but it is none of my business.

The same thing happened with my daughter as I was always watching out for my kids by watching over them. Anyway, I happened to walk in on her one day when she was about 3 years old or so because I heard the bath tub running water nonstop for a while and when I went in to check up on her to make sure she was all right, she was just letting the bathwater run down on her body's special spot where she had positioned herself under the faucet and seemed to be enjoying the event. Because the tub curtain was not closed all the way my daughter did not see me even though I could see her, so I made a sound that got her attention, and asked her if she was all right because I heard the bath water running nonstop for a while and wanted to make sure she was okay. She said that she was fine and I heard the water facet turn off, then I told her that if she enjoyed what she was doing, it was all right for her to continue doing it if what she was doing gave her pleasure. This approach, like the one with my son, ended and that was that. I never did walk in on my daughter again, but that doesn't mean she doesn't still explore herself, but like my son, it is none of my business.

Parents, the reality of one exploring one's body is a natural growth developing process and should never be condemned so as not to instill any negative thought processes in your child's mind. Should children think something is wrong with exploring their own bodies, then parents are asking for trouble some time down the road in the future. In any event parents will be responsible should anything negative happens with any of your children should they become involved in any unusual sexual situation because parents did not know how to act, deal with, or handle these types of situations. In other words, parents, think before you decide to react and use common sense and restrain yourselves before reacting for the benefit of your child or children and remain calm. Something to think about parents is to ask yourselves why we have so many sex stores and major retail outlets promoting and selling all kinds of sexual devices for both men and women for masturbation purposes and for other uses that both men and women can use by themselves or on each other. Likewise, all of this information is being made available for viewing by your child or children on your local television networks, the internet, cell phones, and even being discussed among men to men and women to women. Since there is no shame in using these devices then parents must realize that there is no reason to shame or condemn your child or children when they decide to explore themselves.

Parents, I can't express how important it is the way parents handle these types of situations as the end results can be healthy ones or they can turn out to be unhealthy ones. In my situation, I became obsessed with the female body and went on to learn and understand what pleases women as my desires continued to increase even to this day. However, had my old man took the same approach as I did with my children in this situation, I may have turned out to be a normal guy. Be that as it may, because of my rebellious attitude I was determined to find out and learn what was so bad or wrong about what I was being condemned for because of what I had been doing. Parents, the acts of children discovering and exploring their bodies is nothing more than a learning process for them and should be reasoned with as there is nothing wrong with discovering one's self, and actually it is perfectly normal. What isn't normal is how different people handle these situations as your children develop growing up. Parents, you the ones responsible for how your children will act and view life as they go through it trying to figure out what is and is not right for them.

CHAPTER 14

The Nightmare Gets Worse

As time went on I came to find out that this little town of Clawson in Michigan we moved to had a reputation known for thugs, gangs, rapes, murders and burglaries and other crimes. What a great place for a family to move to not knowing what they were getting involved with even though the old man was from Michigan. I am sure or at least I thought that the old man figured that he could deal with this community as small as it was in 1959, but what he didn't realize was that small towns grow up to become bigger towns. Anyways, I was starting in the 3rd grade in school only to discover that these kids back East were way ahead of what we had been learning in Arizona out West; these kids were already reading and writing and I only knew how to print words the way I was taught in the third grade in the Arizona school system. Technically, this should have not have been a problem, but in reality it became a major problem for me because I was held back a year and had to learn all over again a second time in the third grade in order to read and write before I could advance to the next grade.

The bad part about this situation was that my parents didn't even think about getting adequate outside help for me in order to assist me in learning how to read and write so that I could advance to the 4th grade with the other kids. Although my parents did take me to a feckless teacher who was making extra money tutoring kids after school from another school district. In any event on the very first day with this so-called teacher I got stuck on the word "ON," and for some unknown reason I could not pronounce this word no matter how hard I tried. Despite that this teacher refused to tell me the word and we ended up wasting a whole hour together. When my old man arrived, this feckless teacher told the old man that I was not capable of learning and that she did not want to tutor me anymore; yet, she didn't tell the old man what an incompetent feckless teacher she was. Parents have no idea how devastating and embarrassing it is to a child's physic to be held back in school for a year just because other school systems do not teach the same curriculums all across the country at the same grade levels back then. Unfortunately for me, the results were catastrophic, crippling, detrimental, traumatic, and disastrous toward my overall mental development, not to mention what I now thought about teachers and my attitude towards them. This was the point in my life where everything started changing for me in school, as well as, my home life and my parents were just as bad when it came to my situation. To my old man, I was now a dumb stupid person who would never be able to accomplish anything and to my mother I was considered to be handicapped with little mental abilities. Hence, the black sheep in the family and to say I was outraged would be an understatement. Basically, I lost all interest in learning anything in the academic world because I was told by my parents that I would never amount to anything, so, why should I bother learning?

Fortunately for me, I maintained physical attributes that now put me a full physical development year ahead of the other kids and if any of them attempted to bother me, I would immediately put them down and in their place physically if I had to. Needless to say, very few if any other kids attempted to bother me and once I had learned this, I realized that I could control other kids and use them to get whatever I desired. Very rapidly I learned how to manipulate different kids and get them to do what I wanted and they all went right along with my directions. On the other side of this equation were the enemies known as parents and teachers that I would have to eventually deal with in time. My second third grade teacher was okay, but I had little respect for teachers and I had no desire to learn any school junk and mostly played with the girls all day in class. However, I did manage to learn enough to get by and was passed through the other grades having a very poor grade average, but hey, like I really cared.

In my second year in the 3rd grade I had been acting up in class one day and the teacher asked me to come out in the hall where she slapped me across the face only because she saw my old man hit me, so she thought she could to the same thing to me and then she told me to behave. In response, I simply said that I had to go to the bathroom and then left the school and went somewhere else to play until school was out, at which time I went home. However, the one thing that I learned was that using the bathroom excuse was now a way out of the classroom until one day the female Principal decided to enter the boys' bathroom where I was learning to smoke, and she took me to her office and told me to bend over her desk and attempted to try and paddle me. Unfortunately for her, I turned and struck her in the chest as hard as I could knocking her down and knocking the air out of her even though she was an old lady, and as I went in for the kill the school janitor just happened to be going by the office and came to her rescue. Immediately, I again left the principal's office and left the school grounds and went home when school was out. The reason I didn't think anything about hitting the principal, teacher, or anyone else for that matter was due to my old man who had told all 4 of us boys that no one had a right to put their hands on us for any reason, other than him, and if they did, we had the old man's permission to do whatever it takes to get away from whomever it was who was trying to hit or harm us in anyway and to me this included principals and teachers. The one thing I should point out to the reader was that I never developed an attacking attitude, but whenever anyone ever took or takes an aggressive action towards me, I did develop an unrelenting retaliation of physical or verbal aggression until the other person gave up, retreated, or I got even with them one way or another, and I show no mercy towards the other person until they are subdued.

The bad part about this incident was that my parents were called by the school principal, were told what took place, and told my parents that I would not be allowed back in school unless I had a psychological evaluation. No problem, a few days later we were off to the University of Michigan for a psych eval, which I knew nothing about because my parents thought it best not to tell me at that time. The psych eval took several hours and I was submitted to all kinds of tests, analytical, logical, and other tests. After about 4 or 5 hours and several people later I was escorted into the head guy's office who asked me a lot more questions and finally stated that they felt that I should be kept and held over at their psych facility for additional testing, apparently looking for some kind of reaction from me that would indicate that I needed additional psychological help for having such a violent disposition. Knowing that these people did not have my analytical and logical thinking abilities, I simply responded with "If that is what you people think, then it is okay with me." Needless to say, they immediately released me back into my parents custody and away we went back home. However, what I didn't know at the time and didn't find out until years later, was that the University of Michigan's psychic department had called my school and told them that there was no problem allowing me back into school and that they would be sending their findings in a report in a week or two. So, back to school I went.

Parents, we have all heard the cliché that states, "What you don't know won't hurt you," well, in my case it was true. When the report came back from the University, it turned out that I maintained a high IQ. The school I was attending was told that the problem with me was that they were not teaching me fast enough and, therefore, was contributing to my boredom and lackadaisical attitude, which to me was not true and made absolutely no sense to me anyways. Talk about stunned, these people including my own parents could not understand why with my analytical and logical thought abilities that was assessed by the University of Michigan's Psychological Division could cause such an unenthusiastic and a couldn't-care-less attitude about school. However, not once was I ever asked, or told about this situation, or how, or why I was lethargic, apathetic and unconcerned about things going on around me, especially, with school work. Here I am years later figuring out that these feckless teachers thought they knew what was best for me and little did they know that there would be nothing they could do for me that would turn me around or change my attitude. All the damage to me had already been done by my parents by the way they had raised me in my early childhood years.

PART 2

The Nightmare

Continues

This time the old cliché that states, "What you don't know can't hurt you," got turned around on me because it seemed everyone else, meaning my parents and the teachers, either heard or knew about the results of my psychic eval while I was kept in the dark. Since our old man had a 4th grade education back in the early 1900s, it was more important for him to work in his dad's Tool and Die business instead of going to school. My mother on the other hand had graduated from Bowling Green University in Ohio, so there was a major educational difference between my two parents and yet neither one of them knew anything about raising children other than the way their were raised. Nevertheless, my parents and teachers having this information managed to make my life even more miserable; why? I can only guess, but I believed that my old man felt threatened by my intellect and my mother just couldn't understand why I was doing so poorly in school including the teachers. Again, no one even tried to ask me any questions concerning these situations in an attempt to get my viewpoints, which told me that no one cared one way or another about what I thought, so why should I care and I continued to do poorly in school because that was what was expected of me.

Finally, I managed to pass the third grade or rather the school system just wanted to get me out of 3rd grade since this was the least path of resistance, so I made it to the 4th grade. This is where I ran into the best teacher that I ever had in all of my school years. She was kind, polite, concerned, and interested in all of her students and, especially, me; why and for what reason I have no idea other than she was a great teacher. Under this teacher's tutelage my desire to learn started manifesting itself in me and I started developing a desire for math and reading, but I never did grasp English grammar and spelling very well as it seemed monotonous to me at the time, and besides, I could always look up any word I needed in a dictionary. Anyways, the fourth grade set me on a path that would eventually lead me to getting a Master's Degree in Finance in Business Administration after having received a Bachelor's in Business Management via the internet just for my own satisfaction. However, because of some very poor teachers and other outside retired teachers that managed to destroy any desire I may have had towards learning anything in English, I am still a very poor speller even to this day, but I managed to get my points across, so, who cares. These days I just write books and invest in the stock market, but had I had teachers like the one I had in the 4th grade, there would be no telling where or what I could have achieved in the academic world.

The Fifth, Sixth, Seventh, and Eight grades were a waste of my time because I had no teachers that seemed to be interested in anything other than their own interest. If their students learned something or not, these so-called feckless teachers just passed and pushed the kids along to the next grade. In my opinion, these teachers were nothing more than feckless varlets collecting a paycheck because they were not qualified to hold a job in the real world other than the job they currently had. Parents, these are the teachers that are brainwashing your children and it is your job to question these teachers when they have parent-teacher conferences. Parents need to start vetting these teachers to see if they meet your expectations for your children's education, and if they don't, talk to the principal and request that your child be moved to another classroom. Parents, you need to know that teachers can be very destructive to your children in the way they present subject matter to them because your children's minds are an open slate that can be manipulated and influenced anyway a teacher desires. For those readers who don't believe what was just stated, just look around at our society today and view these rioters and protesters all across America and ask yourself where did these people learn what to riot and protest about? Answer:

From teachers who have brainwashed them in our school and college systems along with the other kids. Moving on to high school, my parents decided like they did with my older brother to send me to military school to supposedly teach us why, when, where, and how to study or at least that is what our old man told us that absolutely made no sense to me. I thought that is what we were supposed to be learning in our school system, but apparently not. Anyways, I managed to get kicked out of the military academy in less than six months for fighting, and this event caused a problem as the high school I was attending decided that they didn't want me back in their school. However, the school administrators told my parents that they would allow me to attend the last six weeks of the school year, but I had to make the honor roll in order to pass, and my parents agreed. Even though I didn't know about this condition this was fine for me because I would get a break from school for most of the rest of the school year, not that I would have learned anything by going back to high school in the first place, but my parents didn't tell me about the agreement they had made with the high school. Nonetheless, I ended up staying at home and going to the bowling ally with my mother who was in a women's bowling league. Boy, talk about insipid, there is nothing worse than listening to a bunch of cackling women doing nothing but gossiping and making a lot of noise deciding who was going to get the next word in edgewise in whatever they were talking about.

After about a month of going with my mother to the bowling ally every week, I decided that I needed to do something else constructive, like teaching myself how to drive. To me this was a good idea so I devised a plan that would allow me to take my mother's car and go drive around for a while to teach myself how to drive without anyone knowing anything about it. The following week at the bowling ally an opportunity presented itself to me in which my mother would be tied up for a while so I got her keys out of her purse and took the car. First I drove over to a friend's home and when he wasn't home, I backed out of the driveway and barely missed hitting a telephone pole. Anyways, I decided to drive over to our school only to find out that everyone was in school so I made my way back to the bowling ally. When I arrived at the bowling ally, someone else had parked in the same parking space that my mother had parked in, so I just parked in another space in the same front space only one row over. When I got back in the bowling ally, all I had to do was replace my mother's keys in her purse and I would be home safe and sound as if nothing had ever happened. When it came time to leave, my mother noticed that the car wasn't in the same parking space and I told her she must be mistaken unless one of her girl friends moved it. She must have bought my explanation as we then departed the bowling ally.

For the next couple of weeks everything seemed to be going okay when the old man got home one day and called for me, asking me why I had stolen his car and went driving around the high school. Being completely dumb founded that he knew this or how he even found out about it, I figured that he would just beat the day likes out of me as usual and that would be the end of that, boy, was I wrong. Actually the old man didn't beat me and instead grounded me for the rest of the year and took away my allowance. Not that my allowance was a big deal as I only got .50 cents a week and I had to save half of it. Since this reaction was really unusual for the old man, I didn't question his motives and just acquiesced to his demands without receiving any further explanations.

In spite of this incident with my old man, I was approaching the last six weeks of high school before being let out for summer break, and only then did my parents tell me the terms that they had agreed to with the school administrators when I returned to school. Boy, talk about being taken by surprise, this was something that I could have never anticipated, but hey, no problem, I'd just go ahead and make the honor roll and that would be the end of that or so I thought. When school finals were over and everyone saw my name posted on the high school honor roll list that was posted on various walls in the high school, the whole ninth grade student body was shocked including all the teachers. Not that any of this bothered me, but I had just created a major problem for myself because everyone including my parents now new that I had been faking stupidity all of my years in school, but, hey, who cared anyways, certainly not me.

Moving on to the Tenth grade I got into it with one of the teachers and after his head shattered the glass window in the classroom door I got expelled from high school even though the teacher caused the problem. We were in History class when this halfwit teacher came up behind me and hit me in the back of my head with a History book because he thought I had been talking, which I wasn't. Unfortunately, this teacher immediately got my full attention and when he walked by me, I retaliated by pushing him towards the front of the class and when he turned around towards me, I again pushed him as hard as I could and his head shattered the glass window that was in the door. All I was doing was getting even with him for him hitting me in the back of my head for no reason. Despite the fact that this feckless teacher was in the wrong, I was the one who got thrown out of high school and nothing happened to this teacher simply because I retaliated to get even with this dimwit. Needless to say this event ended my high school years and I was put into the military by my parents where I earned a GED diploma, not that getting a GED was any big deal, but so much for finishing high school.

CHAPTER 15

More To Come

Over time things seemed to calm down until the old man decided to take a trip to Wisconsin taking the old lady with him and leaving me in the hands of my older brother, another fatal parental mistake. Anyways, the parents left and I was trying to convince my older brother to let me out of the house to play and while he continued to refuse my ongoing requests, I had to devise a plan to get him to let me go do the things I wanted to do. Finally, I decided to get the old man's BB gun out of the closet when my older brother saw me, and he took the BB gun from me and started playing with it pointing it at various objects. However, sometimes the gun worked and sometimes it just kept misfiring, and my brother decided to point the BB gun at my head and fired. Again, the gun missed fired so he pointed the barrel down at my knee and fired, only this time a BB came out striking me in the knee and now I knew that I had the leverage against my older brother as I swore to tell the old man what he did to me.

Even though the BB hurt like heck and I continued to make a lot of noise that scared my older brother enough for him to cave-in to my demands and he told me that I could go out, but not to tell our old man and away I went as free as a bird. For the next couple of days everything was going great when suddenly I ran across one of our gang members who told me where I could get my hands on a car. So we met the person and all he wanted in exchange for the car was a radio he had seen in a certain store in town. After making a deal to trade him the radio for using his car for a couple of hours, I immediately went to the store and stole the radio as I had become a very proficient thief and had never been caught. At the time I had no idea of what a 1966 Corvair was, but I traded the radio for the car and away we went for a couple of hours of fun, or so we thought. We drove all over the town that night having a blast, but on our way back to return the car and as luck would have it, we got stopped by the police and I was hauled off to jail while they let my buddy go free. Nevertheless, the cops had to call my brother who had to come down and get me out of jail after they had issued me a ticket for driving without a license. Just great, as the old man and old lady would be back in another couple of days and I would be beaten again. When the parents returned, we told them that everything was fine, but the old man somehow knew better and started questioning us as to what may have happened while they were gone and again we said nothing that would set the old man off. The only problem was that I had an appearance date in court that my parents would have to take me to. So, a couple of days later I ended up telling the old man and showing him the ticket and again he did nothing to me. Also, he did nothing to my older brother who I told to tell our old man that I snuck out of the house without my brother having any knowledge of it or where I was at the time. The main reason the old man did nothing to me was because we had to go to court and he didn't want them to see me all bruised up, which again I didn't find out until years later.

So off to court we went and the only thing the judge did was to tell me that I would not be allowed to get a driver's license until I turned 17 years old, which was perfectly all right with me, but it never stopped me from stealing cars, only this time I never did get caught again. Parents, you definitely don't need or want a kid like me, and there is so much more deplorable, atrocious, terrible, and corrupt things that I did by myself and with others that the reader doesn't need to know about other than learning how to raise your kids properly and avoid all the headaches, embarrassments, humiliation, and legal problems you could experience by having a stubborn, obstinate, headstrong, iron-willed recalcitrant child like me. How I managed to turn out the way I eventually did, one can only guess, but because the old man became wealthy having stolen from his father and with such little education I had this same internal desire to become even more wealthy than the old man without stealing, along with having an unrelenting drive to prove to the people who knew me that they were completely wrong in their assessments of me, although I never did go back to Clawson, Michigan, to try and see anyone.

Parents should know that even to this day I have no social skills to speak of and I do not care to be around people whatsoever as I am happy and content just the way I am even though I am still a recalcitrant and a borderline curmudgeon all because of the way my parents raised me. Unfortunately, my other three brothers are similar to me even though they spent their time around other people having a complete lack of trust of everyone and anyone except their remaining wives whom they are currently married to. Because of the way we were raised our parents destroyed any chance of us brothers ever having a relationship between us as our old man did his best to turn each of us against each other before he died. We were taught to never trust anyone or accept anything they said at face value and always be on the alert for those who may be trying to take advantage of us or our situation. I even remember my older brother and I being sent out on Halloween nights with baseball bats, while we were still in Michigan in order to prevent any kids attempting to wax or soap the old man's car windows and having his permission to club them if we needed to stop them. Since we were following the old man's orders, it never dawned on us that we could be locked up for doing bodily harm to any kids had we clubbed them for waxing the old man's cars, but that would have been better than getting beaten by the old man again.

As parents you should now understand why the 4 of us boys had a difficult time trying to fit in with other kids while we were growing up because we became very forceful, opinionated, domineering, and uncompromising toward others whether they were kids, teachers, parents, or other people in general. Although all of us boys excelled in all sports like football, basketball, baseball, and myself in hockey, even to the point that my older brother was invited to try out for the Detroit Tigers baseball team, and I got an offer to try out with the Los Angeles Sharks hockey team, there was no reason for us to get along with other people unless it would be to our advantage or benefit us in one way or another as we had no use for them. All of this because of the way we were raised by our parents, but no one ever broke my spirit and since I can't speak for my other 3 brothers, I honestly don't know how their lives have turned out thus far.

To give parents a better idea of what I am talking about, it has been over 50 years since I have spoken with or even seen my youngest brother, it was 30 some years before I saw my next youngest brother, and my oldest brother only because our old man kicked the bucket. In any event the reason the three of us brothers got together was to contest the old man's Will because he had left his entire estate to Children's Hospital and had indicated that he had no children. To add insult to injury, the old man stated in the Will that should his Will be contested that we, my brothers and I, were to be considered dead. What a great dad to have for a parent, but nevertheless we sued, and our little brother's attorney showed up for his cut because he was afraid that we would beat him up if he showed up to contest the old man's Will along with us. It became perfectly clear to us that the old man got into our little brother's head; and all of us received just a pittance of what the estate was valued at when the old man passed away. Since then it has been another 20 or 25 years before I would hear from one of my brothers again because there had been a tragedy that took place with my oldest brother's eldest son who committed suicide, but then again, our eldest brother decided to raise his children the same way our old man raised us. Again, in my opinion, the old way of raising children is no longer a proper or valid way for parents to raise their children in the 21st century and parents need to educate themselves and/or take child rearing courses, or see child professionals who should know how they can help parents and instruct them and teach them a better way to raise their children.

Because we really don't believe parents understand how far a mistreated child can go when they are not raised properly, allow me to give parents another perspective. Years ago in the town of Clawson, Michigan, there was a kid who had been diagnosed and classified as a genius that lived a few blocks from where we were living. Anyways, this kid had a mother that constantly harassed, pressured, and prodded him to always to do better than anyone else because of his intelligence. Unfortunately, one day the kid had gotten fed up and frustrated enough with his mother that he got his father's rifle, went outside and shot and killed his mother through the kitchen window while she had been making dinner for her family. The kid was elated and relieved because he had lifted the burden off of himself even though he was institutionalized for his actions. Parents, situations like this happen all the time and if you push, pressure, physical punish, harass, provoke, and confuse kids, then just like any other animal they will get fed up, turn on you, and bite you one way or another. Incidents like this one are happening more often in today's society than ever before, so, it is wise for a parent or parents to try and find a better way in which to raise your child or children so that you don't become a victim yourself caused by using the old outdated parenting techniques that have been handed down from generations to generations that are now ancient history and have no validity in today's society.

Nevertheless, caution is in order here, because parents should only want to consult with people and professionals that are or have raised children and not just one child as they will be the most qualified to advise, recommend, and offer alternatives so that both of you can give your child the proper attention they may need. There are a lot of so-called professionals and doctors that advertise who have no business being in business and offering feckless advice, so be diligent, meticulous, and deliberate in selecting the right person. If any of these people you interview start to equivocate in anyway, leave and find someone else as it will only benefit you and your child. It is kind of like going to see a divorce counselor who has been divorced to get advice on your marriage situation. In this circumstance the counselor can't help but to reflect back on what happened to him/her during their divorce and their biased opinion will cause them to relate their experience towards their own gender no matter how hard they try to convince you otherwise. So parents, be selective and seek out the most suitable and best counselor you possibly can to help your child because it will definitely be worth it in the long run.

CHAPTER 16

Are Parents Just Bad or Stupid

There are two answers and the first is "Yes" for bad parents and the second is "Yes and No" for stupid parents. Allow me to explain: My idea of bad parents are those parents that everyone else thinks are the perfect parents because they step in to help their children anytime they think something may go wrong that in their minds will hurt their kids. These are the parents that believe they are protecting their children as they grow towards becoming adults. The problem with these kids is that they are being doomed to failure in life because they are never allowed to think for themselves as children. These kids never had to make decisions, embody a multitude of distress and rejections, and experience the dissatisfaction and the reality of failure because their parents protected them at every stage of their developing lives. In essence, these kids grow up not being able to think or function without the supervision of others capable of showing them how, why, when, and where in order for them to do something. More than likely these kids will never amount to anything in the working world unless they have the fortitude to overcome their upbringing and develop an "I can do anything" attitude, but the chances of that happening are slim to none having been raised by bad parents. Sure these kinds of parents can be called by many names, but bad parents are still bad parents. However, there is hope for these kinds of parents, but only if they are willing to learn something new in the coming years concerning raising their children.

Recently I got a call from my daughter in California discussing her daughter and all the praising, acclamation, and admiration comments she and her husband have been receiving concerning their 2-year old from other parents and instructors at her daughter's pre-school because of her independence, intelligence, and her accomplishments. While we were talking my daughter made a statement saying that she and her husband couldn't believe how stupid these other parents were when it came to raising their children. In response, I told my daughter that it is not the fault of these kids' parents, but rather their parents and their parents from generation after generation of their parents. Due to the fact that all these parents had raised their children the same way that their parents raised them and that each past generation had raised each upcoming generation the same way and they just didn't realize that there were better ways to raise their children.

In other words, instead of the parents being stupid, they just never decided to find out that there could be a better way for them to raise their children. Essentially, without looking for a more appropriate way to raise their children, these parents primarily relied on their parenting abilities based on their past experiences that, unfortunately, were based on how they were raised, and it has never entered their thought processes to find a more proficient way to raise children. Inherently, these parents are not stupid people, but they lack the ability to determine a more suitable way for them to raise their children. However, should these parents discover that there is a more advantageous way to raise their children, and they refuse to investigate the legitimacy of such a process, and then refuse and ignore a more desirable child-rearing process, then the answer to the question would definitely be "Yes," they are stupid parents, and, as everyone knows, you can't fix stupid.

Usually, bad parents are the type of parents that do not let their young children out of their homes very much so as not to attract close attention to their children and the atrocities they may be enduring in their home environment. Unless there is serious violence being inflected on a child, it is very difficult to have these kinds of bad parents investigated. That is why the majority of hospitals and general medical offices are told to be on the alert should they suspect that a child brought in for medical care shows any signs of child abuse. In these situations Child Welfare and Protective Services will be called in to ask questions of the parents or in the event of serious damage to a child the police may become involved. The problem with these situations is that the children are usually told by their parents that if their kids should say anything about what happened to them that they will be beat twice as bad, or similar words, the next time or when they come home again. Under these circumstances the children will usually submit to their parents' demands and instead of telling anyone the truth they simply lie as a form of self-preservation; I know because I had to make up stories all the time when I was being raised by my parents. The reason I didn't say anything was because I thought that I would be taken away from my brothers and parents and put into a worse situation than I was currently in, so naturally, I kept my mouth shut.

PART 2

Do Parents Raise Bullies

The answer to this question is most definitely "YES!" Especially, over dominating, physically demanding, or ruling the roost kind of parents, so to speak. More than likely these parents will be the byproduct of parents who were raised the same from generation to generation and now they continue this bad parenting tradition by raising their children using the same old methods, simply because they never looked or tried to find a more adequate way to raise children. When parents do not have or maintain a two-way communication with their children and instead decide to dominate them, this in turn creates a bully that will emerge at one point or another in one form or another during their child's lifetime. This bully syndrome can manifest itself in the form of dominance, violence, needing to be in charge, or having the desire to direct or govern over someone or something in order to release their pent-up hostilities that they have been subjected to and had to endure while they were being raised by these kinds of parents.

The end result of this kind of bully parenting will turn children into bullies simply because the children don't know any better even though they may or may not understand how they became that way. The problem with this situation is that children begin emulating, competing, and rebelling against their parents by taking their frustrations out on others in one form or another by bulling them in order to satisfy their self-esteem and self-worth by getting their way or getting whatever it is that they want by bulling others. In addition, these kids usually lack any respect for others and won't hesitate to confront and stand up to anyone that may disagree with them. Again, this is nothing more than what their parents have been doing to them and now is their time to retaliate against all and anyone who may attempt to exert any authority over them. Parents, just to give you an idea that this can and does happen to children is because my parents made me into one of these kinds of people. Even to this day I maintain absolutely no respect for anyone who attempts to tell me what to do in any shape, manner, or form as I honestly don't care who they are or who they think they are and I will automatically fire back at them in one way or another without thinking.

In any case, parents may be wondering how to break this bulling problem and the only answer we have is to maintain a two-way communication with your children very early in their developing lives by assisting, directing, instructing, and allowing them to make and come to their own decisions and conclusions. This also includes allowing your child or children to be able to communicate to you as their parents what they may think is wrong with the way you are raising them or what they believe you may not be doing for them. Because I was a very determined and authoritative parent which, unfortunately, I still am, even though I have tried my best to change the way I am from the way my parents raised me and my brothers, and even though I managed to change the way I raised my children from the way my brothers and I were raised, there are still a lot of things I could have done better. Unfortunately, parents, we only get one chance at parenthood and we hope all parents everywhere will try to do the best they can and even better for their children unlike the way they were raised.

When my daughter had been in high school a few years, she came home one day and at dinner she lashed out at me verbally wanting to know why I never came to any of her band performances or football games to watch her playing the violin or watching her as a cheerleader. Honestly, I had no answer because I preferred drinking beer (when I used to drink) and what my daughter was asking of me never entered my mind. Nonetheless, I told my daughter that if she would inform me of these events taking place at her school a few days in advance, that I would make it a point to be at these events to watch her. At that time I didn't want to tell my daughter that I had no desire to be around other people because I am not a social person, and I do not like socializing because I don't like people asking me questions about something they have no reason to know about other than for gossiping. The other problem is that the majority of people are feeling people and I am a thinking person having very little if any emotions. For that reason, I avoid people at all costs other than a greeting or so because people frustrate me unless I can learn something from conversing with them. In the aforementioned, I started going to my daughter's events avoiding and ignoring all of the other parents as best as I could as I had no desire to be around them, but I did make my daughter happy and that to me is what counts. Fundamentally, I am a factual person and as long as people are terse and laconic with me and can manage getting to the point in a concise manner then I can usually get along with them. On the other hand, I detest people, especially, women who happen to be longwinded and say things in such a round about manner that technically could be said in a succinct way, short, sweet, and to the point. Notwithstanding, with women this is an impossibility as their right and left brains are developed in such a way that causes them to have the desire to be longwinded, whereas men's left brains are designed to be analytical, systematic, consistent, and organized. Hence, the difference between men and women, only in my case, my analytical and logical brain remains in this stratum for some unknown reason.

What it all gets down to, parents, is plain and simple communication with your children having the understanding, compassion, kindness, sensitivity, and meeting of yours and their minds. For parents to make a bully all they have to do is continue to be harsh, rude, cruel, strict, and hard-hearted by constantly dictating and physically punishing your children. In turn, your children will emulate how they have been raised on others, including their own children should they decide to have a child or children, that they can now take advantage of in the same manner they were being taken advantage of by their parents. As usual, it all reflects back to the parents and the manner in which they decide to raise their children.

What all parents need to understand is that the things they do or say to their child or children will remain with their kids throughout their entire lives and this even includes the little things. For example: All four of us boys were always told that if we were ever sick or hurt that we had better be in a hospital because if we were not the old man would see to it that he would put us in one. Needless to say seldom did any one of us ever get sick and when we got hurt we would go to a hospital only to get sown up or our have our broken bones set. However, when it came to seeing doctors for any other reasons this was completely out of the question and even to this day none of us ever go to see any doctors for any reason unless it is a critical situation. Even thinking about seeing a doctor is out of the question all because of the way we were raised by our parents. Typically, children will become nothing more than definitive reflections and byproducts of their parents and the environment in which they are raised. In spite of all this, the question still remains, will you as a parent become a bad or stupid parent or will you seek a better way of raising your children? Parents, the survival and serendipity of your child or children will only depend on your capabilities, talent, and skillfulness in your parenting abilities that you pass on to your child or children for the benefit of their future.

CHAPTER 17

What Kind of Parents Will you Become

This book has been dedicated to my two wonderful children who were lucky enough to be raised in Southern California the way I thought they should be raised instead of the violent way I was raised back East in Michigan. There is such a difference between the East and West coast parents and how they raise their children, but children are still children and they all deserve to be treated as people from the time they are born until they leave their homes to join our society. A parent or parents should all know and realize that all children are born as a blank slate with a blank computer mind that parents will start programming from the day they are born until they leave your home and hopefully all parents will have done their job correctly, but only time will determine the end results of their upbringing. For those parents who have special children that have been brain damaged at birth for whatever reason, I can only sympathize with you and hope for the best for you and your child because I know first hand what a challenge it will be to assist your special child. If people would like more information concerning their special child or children we recommend contacting "The Institute for the Achievement of Human Potential" in Philadelphia where you can get all the help you may need. The institute also has a large selection of reading and educational materials that anyone can purchase.

As the title of this chapter indicates, "What kinds of parents will you become?"

Current parents, expecting parents, and future parents need to be learning why they must find a better way to raise their children and break out of the old habits the previous generations had of raising children. This is a necessity and a requirement for parents in order to avoid raising future rioters, protesters, delinquents, thieves, rapist, felons, burglars, gunmen, robbers, gangsters, terrorist, or heaven forbid, a killer, or a serial killer just because all of these people were not raised properly when they were children. At one point or another these children experienced an event, an incident, or an occurrence which not have only caught their attention, but whatever happened fascinated them to the point of locking that situation into their brains to be recalled and used by them at a later time in their lives. Certain violent TV programs, violent video games, and video movies, articles about violence on the internet, and other media sources will all have a certain influence on children's brains that can distort their thought processes.

Unfortunately, the majority of children want to be accepted by other kids in their age group and depending on how parents deal with socializing their children with other people and children will also have a major impact on their future lives. For some unknown reason people want to be recognized as if they think they are important for some unknown reason or other. Allow me to point something out to the readers of this book, which I refer to as "Kovach's Laws." People are only important in two places in their lives, I can think of, one of which is their home and the only other place people may be or may not be important is at their place of work. Other than that, no one really cares who you are or what you are, and the same will be applicable concerning your children. Should any readers not believe this is true, just look at how other people treat other people when they are in their vehicles when they think the other person in their vehicle did something they consider was wrong to them for whatever reason. The point being made here is do you think these people care about who you really are while you're in your car or anywhere else in public?

Being the owner and head instructor of the Professional Loan Officers Training Center, I would always ask every student what they thought the word security meant to them on the first day of class. The answers were all over the board from believing that money, jobs, paid off vehicles, owning a home, or whatever else they could think of that seemed important to them, except for the reality, which is from the time you are born until the time you depart from this world, your only security is "Your Health, Your Ability to Think, and Your Ability to Function." Lose just one of these abilities and the rest of your life will be turned upside down. Another one of "Kovach's Laws" I taught my kids was to "Never Assume Anything, Don't Overlook the Obvious, and Don't Create a Problem." This law was mainly designed for the working environment, but can be used in any situation, and when used properly, it can have some amazing results solving problems instead of creating them.

To give the readers an example of the above aforementioned Kovach's Law, when I owned a printing company located in Irvine, California, years ago, I was constantly thinking of better ways to limit the printers movements so that they would keep from getting tired when printing large jobs. My camera operating people, bindery people, and paper cutting people all had limited movement while at their machines, but the printers were constantly going all over the shop to get supplies for the printing presses. So I thought, am I assuming anything, was I overlooking something obvious or was I just creating a problem for the printers and myself? Sitting at my desk thinking, all of a sudden a thought came to my mind that revolved around the concept of the economy of motion. All I had to do now was devise a plan to solve the problem for the printers. After a little reorganizing the printing facility by moving the necessary inks, blanket cleaning chemicals, paper supplies, and almost everything else the printers needed into the printer's working areas, we managed to stop a lot of unnecessary movements for the printers. Now all the printers had to do was pivot on one foot left or right to get the supplies that they needed to complete a printing job. By reorganizing the printers printing areas we managed to limit their movement thereby eliminating excessive movements and as an added bonus we increased printing production and managed to keep the printers happy because now they were no longer getting tired having to run around the shop getting supplies.

Parents, the point being made here is that you should be questioning yourself if you are assuming anything when speaking with your children. Are you, as parents, overlooking the obvious when explaining things to your child or are you creating a problem for not only your kids, but also for yourselves when instructing your children. I found when my children were 5 or 6 years old, I used the "Keep it Simple Stupid" aka "Kiss" method of relating, communicating, and offering advice to my children and they each managed to understand my instructions, dictations, and explanations using this process. Seldom did I ever have to correct my children although I regret not always being around or available for them in their time of need or being able to meet their requests to have my presence at their school events that were important to them at the time they were growing up. The main reason for this was because my parents totally ignored me and my other 3 brothers sporting events and school events when we were growing up. Therefore, I never placed any emphasis or significance on any of their school events that they participated in because of the way we were raised by our parents. Parents, from my perspective try not to disappoint your child or children when it comes to their school activities if at all possible. Unfortunately, I had to learn this lesson the hard way.

CHAPTER 18

The

Bottom Line

What kinds of parents will you become will only be decided by you as the parent. How your child or children eventually turn out will also be determined by you and how your child or children will enter the adult world, will only depend on how well you have raised them. Will your child or children be able to survive in an adult world and become a functional member of our society, or will they be reluctant, shy away, and fail to make the real grade in life? Will your child or children become just another statistic on someone's list or will they excel at whatever they choose to pursue as their career of choice? Will your child or children look forward to the future as a challenge, or will they turn their backs and look for a place to run and hide? Will your child or children honor and respect you as parents or will they despise you for not doing a better job at raising them? Will your child or children look forward to coming home to visit their parents or will they go their own way and ignore their parents? If your child or children have their own children, will your child or children want their own children to know their grandparents or will they decide to keep their children away from their grandparents? All of these questions and many more will be in the minds of your child or children once they leave your home for the last time.

The answers to all of the aforementioned questions will depend on how you as parents raise your children. If your children are raised in an environment where physical contact is being used to control the children, then parents can expect any of the above situations to develop that can be detrimental, damaging, and ruinous for them to ever having a close relationship with their children or their grandchildren, if there are any. On the same side of this coin, parents who use or show violence towards their children in any way, shape, or form can end up having children who grow up to become depressed, despondent, mocked, scorned, or scoffed at, and ridiculed by others because they were never shown any compassion when they were growing up in their own home environment.

Allow me to give parents another example: Recently, I was in a Home Depot looking for a battery hedge trimmer and in the checkout line ahead of us was a parent that had a little boy sitting in the top part of the push cart. The boy appeared to look normal, but seemed to be showing no interest in anything that was going on around him and seemed to be depressed. In spite of that, I decided to ask the boy how old he was and when he didn't respond, his mother instantly told the boy to answer me and he held up three fingers. After congratulating the little boy on reaching the age of 3, I then began conversing with the mother asking her if she or the boy's father ever corrected their child and she immediately responded that they discipline him all the time by hitting his hands and spanking their child. No wonder the little boy was depressed because he was not only embarrassed, humiliated, and confused because he didn't seem to understand why he was being physically punished for whatever it was that he was doing that got him in trouble in the first place.

When I told the mother that they as parents should never put their hands on their child under any circumstances because it may come back on them in the form of some kind of retaliation in the future, she just laughed as she was leaving the store. Parents, these are the typical generation after generation parenting techniques that have been handed down for years. Moreover, this little boy is eventually going to become a failure when he reaches adulthood and will succumb to any and all authority because of the way these stupid parents are raising their child. Will this child become violent, impetuous or ruthless, the likelihood of that happening is not likely because this child's spirit has already been broken. These are the kinds of parents that we are hoping will get and read this book because they need to break the habits of the old way of raising children. On the other hand, this child could grow up to becoming another serial killer or something else just as bad by indirectly getting back at his parents for the way he was being mistreated in his childhood or he could just kill his parents.

On the other side of this coin, you have the more intelligent parents that decide to study and investigate different child rearing information who are willing to change from the old generational syndrome of the child rearing process of physically punishing children just because they think they have a right to do so to learning a better way to raise children. I want to point out again that no one has a right to put their hands on a child in any physical manner whatsoever in my opinion. That is why we have laws that are designed to keep people from physically harming other people, and when they do, they can be arrested, go to court, and if necessary, be placed behind bars where they belong. These laws should also be extended to parents who for some unknown reason physically punish a child. As was stated earlier in this book, if parents are not smart enough to outsmart and outthink their children, then they should never have had any children by accident or otherwise in the first place.

The parents that are willing and have the desire to accept, encourage, challenge, and recognize their children's efforts by offering them lots of approvals with all the love and kindness parents have to offer their children, then have all the children you want or can afford because these kinds of children will enhance our world. These are the types of children that will excel at whatever they decide to do seeking the right opportunities and they will make their parents proud of them. The unity in the family will be richly intensified, amplified, and strengthened for generations to come by incorporating this new way of raising your child or children. Consequently, the bottom line comes down to the responsibility of you, the parent, and the results will be the functionality of your baby to childhood to teen-hood and finally into adulthood.

It should also be pointed out to a parent or parents that this early fetus, baby, and toddler training techniques will last a lifetime with your child or children. However, as your child or children get older and older they will not remember or have any idea of where or how they learned these techniques that were taught to them in the early stages of their lives. Nevertheless, they will instinctively react with the information you taught them automatically and starting at about the age of 5 or 6 they will start remembering what they are currently being taught. Don't take this the wrong way, parents, as there is nothing wrong with how your child or children will react and respond to any given situations in the correct manner that they were instructed by the parent or parents in their beginning childhood years.

All the same, we are just pointing out the facts that kids younger than 5 years of age really don't maintain a conscious memory of what they were taught in their infant and toddler years, but they will react accordingly. The point we are making here is that a parent or parents should not expect to receive any thank youse from their child or children for the early training they have received. All of this early fetus, baby, and toddler training techniques will be for the pure satisfaction, gratification, pride, safety, and fulfillment of the parent or parents that will reward them with the pleasure and enjoyment of knowing that you have done your jobs exceedingly well. Notwithstanding, as your child or children approach their adolescence years they will be happy and content knowing that they have reliable and responsible parents that they can rely on who have taught and trained them well.

CHAPTER 19

The Realities of Being

A

Parent

What parents need to realize is that they are parents, which means, that they are Instructors, Trainers, Educators, Mentors, Confidants, Counselors, Guardians, Advisors, and a whole slew of other classifications. However, parents are not your child or children's best friends, companion or soulmates. Therefore, it is the parents job to program your child or children's minds in such a way as to prepare and train them to be able to function in the future so that they become productive individuals. Using the methods in this book or any other alternative methods of raising children in a loving, kind, respectful, and considerate home environment, without physical violence, will reward parents for years to come. Furthermore, this should make parents proud and gratified to witness the development from their child's infant stage through adulthood concerning the overall growth of the child or children you have been raising and preparing to become constructive, effective, worthwhile, and valuable members of our society.

Recently, we read several articles on the internet regarding divorced women, indicating why they became burned out trying to be "Super Moms" for their child or children that only ended up destroying their marriages. Parents, trying to be super moms or dads is a social myth and a fallacy that parents have to get out of their thought processes or they will become the reason for their families' failure. Facts: There is no such thing as super moms or dads when it comes to your child or children. As long as moms are efficient, systematic, methodical, productive, positive, and consistent with your child or children you will be a great parent. As for dads, they should also maintain the same characteristics as their wives, in addition to being logical, orderly, effective, competent, stable, and reliable because you will be the foundation in any marriage that will also make you a great parent. Should any parent try to be anything else to their child or children, they will be asking for trouble, problems, and possible burn out that may lead to the demise of your marriage had one or both of you not tried to be super parents to your child or children. Taking situations in stride as they develop will keep both parents from becoming frustrated parents having the tendency of venting your frustration by striking out at your child or children verbally or physically. In any event, either way parents may decide to react towards their kids under these circumstances will definitely be the wrong way, and parents could face long term repercussions from your child or children, not to mention the damage you may have caused to your child or children's thought processes. When parents become frustrated or discombobulated with their child or children, the best thing we recommend is to walk away from the problem or situation until you have had time to regain your composure and have analyzed the problem or situation from a different perspective. Remember, your job as parents is to outthink and out-smart your child or children and not to hurt them or harm them verbally or physically under any circumstances.

The best way to avoid any of these situations is to train your child or children as early as possible including while they are developing in the womb or as soon after birth as possible. As we have stated before, this early training will remain with your child or children throughout their lifetime. Starting as early as parents can will not only benefit the child, but it will benefit the parents by making parenting simple instead of hectic, frantic, and furious. If parents find themselves in these circumstances, it can cause parents to experience anxieties, possible panic attacks, depression, and several other side affects that can affect the overall mental abilities and the stability of the parents. On the other hand, by making parenting simple, calm, leisurely, gentle, and comfortable as it should be, parents will be fulfilling their roles as good parents and receive a lifetime of enjoyment from their child or children and, eventually, their possible grandchildren.

Granted that the parents who elect to train their children in the womb or start immediately after birth will be the parents that will be the recipients of parenting made simple and will have the advantage over the other parents who have a child or children over the age of 3 to about the age of 6, or before the kids begin kindergarten and become under the influence of the school teachers. Nonetheless, these older children can still be taught and trained by their parents, but only if the parents really want to change the way they have been discipling and training their child or children. Up until this point in their children's lives parents may have been correcting and disciplining their children by yelling, screaming, or hollering, or physically hurting them in one way or another. Be it as it may, somehow reality has entered these parents thought process telling them that their old way of raising children is not the proper way because everything they have been doing to their child or children has had no effectiveness. That being the case, parents wanting or deciding to change their parenting techniques must realize that it will require a considerable amount of time, patience, and effort on their behalf, and the sooner they start the better their chances are that their child or children will adapt to this new parenting approach and strategy being incorporated by their parents. Parents also have to realize that in order to be effective they must be consistent in their parental training. Remember parents, you are dealing with a more mature brain developed children from 3 to 6 years of age that have been suppressed by their parents because of bad parenting techniques. The turnabout of parenting techniques may require the same amount of time in order to undo the damage that may have already been done to their children's brains and thought processes. In addition, parents must realize that the closer your children are to entering the school system you will now be competing with school propaganda that the teachers will be indoctrinating your kids to.

Parents may now understand why it is imperative for them to start as early as possible training their child or children that they may bring into this world. The future of our society is depending on your parenting abilities and, hopefully, the child or children you decide to raise will also be relying on you as their parents to raise them in a loving and caring manner for both of your benefits. So, we will say it again;

"What Kind of Parent Will You Become?"

Good Luck and May All Parents Everywhere Raise Their

Child or Children With

Love, Kindness, and The Respect They All Deserve.

Additional Books Published By The Author

For those of you that may be interested, Mr. Kovach has produced one of the most detailed home buying books on the market now in its second edition entitled **"Home Buying & Financing 101—Second Edition."** He has also published a retirement book that technically can benefit everyone and anyone regardless of their age. However, this book is mostly an autobiography about the author and his wife and what went through having only eight years to get ready for retirement and having no savings to retire on and how they overcame this problem. The second part in this book has some very valuable information on how people can save and live within their means or below their means and is entitled **"How Anyone Can Retire Living Large on Pennies."** In addition, Mr Kovach has also produced another book called **"How To Establish One's Credit"** in addition to a section on **"How To Negotiate on Anything"** thereby allowing people to save thousands of dollars. All 3 books can either be read as an E-book or ordered in a paperback copy format and can be viewed on Kindle or bought on Amazon. Note: The credit book is also in the BONUS section in the Second Edition of the Home Buying & Financing Book minus the "How To Negotiate on Anything" section. However, "How To Negotiate on Anything" is included in the BONUS section of the "How Anyone Can Retire Living Large on Pennies" book, but either way, if one would like to own or read these subject matters, they can be bought or viewed on Amazon or Kindle.

Thank You For Your Time

www.ingramcontent.com/pod-product-compliance
Lightning Source LLC
Chambersburg PA
CBHW070453100426
42743CB00010B/1605